A NEW

SCULP

TURA

LISM

A NEW SCULPTURALISM

Contemporary Architecture from Southern California

Organized by Christopher Mount

Skira *RIZZOLI*
NEW YORK

in association with the Museum of Contemporary Art, Los Angeles

Published with the assistance of the Getty Foundation

This publication accompanies the exhibition "A New Sculpturalism: Contemporary Architecture from Southern California," organized by Christopher Mount and presented at the Museum of Contemporary Art, Los Angeles, the Geffen Contemporary at MOCA, June 2–September 2, 2013.

"A New Sculpturalism: Contemporary Architecture from Southern California" is part of Pacific Standard Time Presents: Modern Architecture in L.A.

AN INITIATIVE OF THE GETTY

The Getty

Major support of the exhibition is provided by the Getty Foundation.

Generous support is provided by the Graham Foundation for Advanced Studies in the Fine Arts.

Additional support is provided by Hagy and Jane Belzberg.

Publications Manager: Elizabeth Hamilton
Project Editor: Holly La Due
Photo Editor: Jennifer Park
Designer: Michael Worthington with Ania Diakoff at Counterspace, Los Angeles
Custom lettering designed by Micah Hahn

2013 2014 2015 2016 10 9 8 7 6 5 4 3 2 1
First published in the United States of America in 2013 by

Skira Rizzoli Publications, Inc.
300 Park Avenue South
New York, NY 10010
www.rizzoliusa.com

In association with
The Museum of Contemporary Art, Los Angeles
250 South Grand Avenue
Los Angeles, CA 90012
www.moca.org

ISBN-13: 978-0-8478-4011-3

Library of Congress Control Number: 2012953897

Front cover
Morphosis Architects, Diamond Ranch High School, Pomona, California, 1999
Pages 2–3
Gehry Partners, Walt Disney Concert Hall, Los Angeles, 2003
Page 4
XTEN Architecture, Nakahouse, Los Angeles, 2010
Page 5
Bestor Architecture, Floating Bungalow, Los Angeles, 2009
Page 7
Ball-Nogues Studio, *Maximilian's Schell*, installation at Materials & Applications, Los Angeles, 2005
Page 8
Patrick Tighe Architecture, Tigertail Residence, Los Angeles, 2008
Page 9
Warren Techentin Architecture, Los Feliz Residence 1, Los Angeles, 2008
Page 10
Belzberg Architects, Los Angeles Museum of the Holocaust, Los Angeles, 2010
Page 11
Eric Owen Moss Architects, Samitaur Tower, Culver City, California, 2010
Page 12
B + U, Frank and Kim Residence, Pasadena, California, 2010
Page 13
Daly Genik Architects, Art Center College of Design South Campus, Pasadena, California, 2004
Page 14
Daly Genik Architects, Palms House, Los Angeles, 2011
Page 16
P-A-T-T-E-R-N-S, Prism Gallery, West Hollywood, California, 2009
Page 17
Belzberg Architects, Skyline Residence, Los Angeles, 2007
Pages 18–19
Daly Genik Architects, Camino Nuevo High School, Los Angeles, 2006
Page 21
Grinstein/Daniels Architects, Kentucky Fried Chicken Restaurant, Los Angeles, 1990
Page 22
Office of Greg Lynn FORM, Los Angeles, 2012
Page 24
Eric Owen Moss Architects, What Wall?, Culver City, California, 1998
Page 25
Morphosis Architects, Caltrans District 7 Headquarters, Los Angeles, 2004
Page 26
Daly Genik Architects, Winnett, Santa Monica, California, 2007
Page 27
Morphosis Architects, Diamond Ranch High School, Pomona, California, 1999

Contents

Foreword

"A New Sculpturalism: Contemporary Architecture from Southern California" surveys important Los Angeles architecture of the past twenty-five years, identifying key firms and practitioners whose works have not only distinguished this city as a locus for experimentation, but have also influenced design internationally. Across a variety of projects, the exhibition traces the common thread of *sculpturalism*—the emphasis on an expressiveness of form that breaks away from the modernist ideals that have heavily influenced regional architecture since the 1920s. Tying the sculpturalist aesthetic to the character of Los Angeles—its history, its opportunities, and its particular zeitgeist—"A New Sculpturalism" identifies this significant development in architecture as an integral component of Los Angeles' artistic and cultural milieu, highlighting work by the many firms that have risen to prominence here since the mid-1980s.

Significantly, "A New Sculpturalism" is presented at the museum's Geffen Contemporary building (formerly the Temporary Contemporary), a police-car warehouse in Little Tokyo that was renovated by Frank O. Gehry in 1983. One of the most significant architects working today, Gehry initiated the revolutionary approach to design that the exhibition celebrates, and his work is featured throughout. Over the years, the Museum of Contemporary Art, Los Angeles (MOCA), has organized a handful of shows that have focused on Gehry's designs, including "Walt Disney Concert Hall: A Celebration of Music and Architecture" (1996), which previewed his plans for the new home of the Los Angeles Philharmonic, and "Frank O. Gehry: Work in Progress" (2003), which coincided with the hall's completion and featured sketches, photographs, and models of a range of projects by way of illustrating his design process.

MOCA has also shown a long-standing commitment to surveying the international terrain of architecture and urbanism, and "A New Sculpturalism" extends the museum's mission to keep abreast of developments in architecture and design and their impact on social, cultural, and economic life. In 1994, MOCA presented "Urban Revisions: Current Projects for the Public Realm," which featured proposals conceived to challenge accepted strategies of urban architecture and planning, examining the issues raised by each. "Blueprints for Modern Living: History and Legacy of the Case Study Houses" (1989) examined *Arts & Architecture* magazine's landmark Case Study House program and its influence on contemporary architecture around the world. In 2000, MOCA mounted the ambitious survey "At the End of the Century: One Hundred Years of Architecture," a comprehensive global accounting of twentieth-century architecture from the vantage point of the turn of the millennium, with a special focus on the profound impact of technology on architecture and urban planning. "Skin and Bones: Parallel Practices in Fashion and Architecture" (2006) explored the common visual and intellectual principles that underlie fashion and architectural design. MOCA has also chronicled the history of Los Angeles architecture, exploring the legacy of key figures including Rudolph Schindler, Richard Meier, and Robert Venturi. Many of the practitioners featured in "A New Sculpturalism" have been at the center of solo exhibitions or special projects at MOCA, including Ball-Nogues Studio, Gehry, and Franklin D. Israel.

"A New Sculpturalism" is the second MOCA exhibition to be funded as part of the Getty Foundation's multiyear Pacific Standard Time initiative celebrating art and architecture in Southern California. It follows "Under the Big Black Sun: California Art 1974–1981," organized by former MOCA Chief Curator Paul Schimmel and presented in 2011. We are once again honored to have been chosen to stand alongside so many of Southern California's prestigious cultural institutions as part of Pacific Standard Time Presents: Modern Architecture in L.A. I am exceedingly grateful to guest exhibition curator Christopher Mount for developing the project and bringing it to MOCA. Mount has a deep and abiding passion for Los Angeles architecture past and present, and his rigor in tracing sculpturalism's myriad, tangled influences has made this exhibition and catalogue a significant addition to the existing scholarship. Thanks also to Research Assistant Johanna Vandemoortele for her tremendous efforts in assisting with the exhibition's organization.

For its endorsement of this exhibition as part of Pacific Standard Time Presents: Modern Architecture in L.A., I extend utmost thanks to the J. Paul Getty Trust, especially James Cuno, president and chief executive officer. For its crucial funding support and the contributions of staff overseeing the grants, I thank the Getty Foundation, especially Deborah Marrow, director; Joan Weinstein, deputy director; Anne Helmreich, senior program officer; Dana Hutt, program assistant; and Kathleen Johnson, project manager, for their steadfast commitment to this and all the Pacific Standard Time Presents projects. Thanks also go to the Getty Research Institute for taking on an important advisory role during the organization of the exhibition, especially Wim de Wit, head, Department of Architecture and Contemporary Art; Christopher James Alexander, assistant curator of architecture and design, Department of Architecture and Contemporary Art; Ann Harrison, senior special collections cataloger, Collections Management; and Rani Singh, principal project specialist in the Department of Architecture and Contemporary Art.

"A New Sculpturalism" was supported by a generous grant from the Graham Foundation for Advanced Studies in the Fine Arts. I especially thank Graham Foundation Director Sarah Herda on behalf of MOCA for her support of the project. I am also grateful to Hagy and Jane Belzberg for their generous contribution. I once again extend deepest thanks to MOCA's extraordinary Board of Trustees, especially Founding Chair Eli Broad; Maria Arena Bell, co-chair; David G. Johnson, co-chair; Jeffrey Soros, president; and Fred Sands, vice chair. Their inspired leadership and unwavering commitment to the museum has made this and many other important exhibitions possible.

Finally, I thank the architects both for their inspired work and their generous participation in this exhibition. They have opened their archives, given their time, and shared their ideas, as well as parted with important documentation related to the extraordinary work surveyed in this exhibition. Los Angeles continues to be an important international center for architecture and design because of their ambitious and visionary contributions.

Jeffrey Deitch, Director
The Museum of Contemporary Art, Los Angeles

Acknowledgments

The exhibition "A New Sculpturalism: Contemporary Architecture from Southern California" is the first to examine the enormous creative explosion that has occurred in the field of architecture in Los Angeles during the past twenty-five years. This exhibition would not have been possible without the enthusiasm and support of Jeffrey Deitch, director of the Museum of Contemporary Art, Los Angeles (MOCA), who immediately embraced the premise of the project and understood its value to Los Angeles and its culture. "A New Sculpturalism" takes its place as part of the rich history of architecture exhibitions at MOCA, and I am grateful to those who have organized previous shows for setting such a high standard for this endeavor.

Generous support has come from the Getty Foundation for "A New Sculpturalism," which is part of its Pacific Standard Time Presents: Modern Architecture in L.A. initiative. I am grateful to J. Paul Getty Trust Director Deborah Marrow for her guidance and to Deputy Director Joan Weinstein and Senior Program Officer Anne Helmreich for their wonderful support and contributions. For conceiving the program I thank my friend and colleague Wim de Wit, head of the Department of Architecture and Contemporary Art at the Getty Research Institute, and assistant curator of architecture and design Christopher James Alexander. I also offer my sincere thanks to Getty Research Institute Senior Special Collections Cataloguer Ann Harrison, Project Manager Kathleen Johnson, Deputy Director Andrew Perchuk, and Principal Project Specialist Rani Singh.

I am exceedingly grateful for the sponsorship that has come from the Graham Foundation, and thank Graham Foundation Director Sarah Herda on behalf of MOCA for her support. A debt of gratitude is owed as well to Hagy and Jane Belzberg for their contribution to "A New Sculpturalism."

This endeavor would not have been possible without the thoughtful and considerate advice of the advisory committee members, who gave liberally of their time to help shape the exhibition and publication from its inception. They include Frances Anderton, Margaret Crawford, Edward Dimendberg, Paul Goldberger, John Kaliski, Matilda McQuaid, Sam Lubell, Nicholas Olsberg, and Nicolai Ouroussoff. A great deal of thanks also goes to the architects participating in this exhibition, not only for their remarkable designs but also for being so cooperative during the planning stages. They made years of archived projects available to us to sift through and learn from. In addition to the principals, I am grateful to those who worked hard to supply much of the information, images, and content for this exhibition, including Anisa Aboutalebpour, Matt Bean, Ashley Coon, Donna Clandening, Ian Dickerson, Meara Daly, Christine Denari, Natalie Egnatchik, Lindsay Erickson, Emily Hodgdon, Alyssa Holmquist, Erin Kasimow, Jen Lathrop, Kristofer Leese, Eric Leishman, Sabina Lira, Meaghan Lloyd, Manzer Mirkar, Eric McNevin, Daniele Profeta, Genevieve Pepin, Allison Porterfield, Joyce Shin, Legier Stahl, and Andrea Tzvetkov.

This beautiful catalogue owes its existence to a very talented team of collaborators. At MOCA, I am most thankful to Senior Editor and Publications Manager Elizabeth Hamilton, who oversaw all aspects of the publication, for her careful attention to the texts and for making mine actually enjoyable to read. Photo Editor Jennifer Park worked tirelessly to procure all the images and image rights. At Skira Rizzoli, I am thankful to Publisher Charles Miers for supporting this project and to Architecture Editor Dung Ngo, Associate Publisher Margaret Chace, and Project Editor Holly La Due for shepherding the book to completion. I also am grateful to writers Margaret Crawford, Sam Lubell, Nicholas Olsberg, and Johanna Vandemoortele, who have shared their expertise to help make this book an important scholarly work. Most significantly, I want to thank Michael Worthington for his beautiful catalogue design and his inexhaustible patience in working with us to achieve it.

An exhibition like this is often a kind of exercise in contemporary archaeology that produces eclectic material to install. My gratitude goes to Annie Chu and Rick Gooding, principals of Chu + Gooding, and their staff, Karena Auseth, Enoch Chow, and Michael Matteucci, for their masterful exhibition design, which is an elegant and inventive solution to a difficult installation. I am also grateful to the entire MOCA staff for their unwavering support and hard work—they have all been instrumental in this exhibition's success. My most heartfelt thanks go to Research Assistant Johanna Vandemoortele, who has proved to be a valued colleague and collaborator. She has worked tirelessly, with enthusiasm, intelligence, and humor, to see this project to fruition. With grace and composure she has kept this sometimes chaotic project under control. I am also grateful to Chief Financial Officer Michael Harrison, who has overseen all financial aspects of the show, and to Exhibition Coordinator Susan Jenkins for her kind and intelligent advice and oversight. Co-Directors of Development Jill Haynie and Veridiana Pontes-Ring and Assistant Director of Development for Institutional Giving Kris Lewis helped garner critical financial support for the exhibition; Director of Exhibition Production Jang Park and Exhibition Production Coordinator Stacie B. London executed the beautiful installation; Registrar Rosanna Hemerick and Associate Registrar Sandy Choi ensured that all the objects in the exhibition arrived safely; and Director of Education Catherine Arias pulled together a thought-provoking slate of exhibition-related programs for the public. Former Chief Curator Paul Schimmel, former Senior Curator Philipp Kaiser, Senior Curator Alma Ruiz, Curator Bennett Simpson, and Associate Curator Rebecca Morse were very supportive curatorial colleagues. Thanks also go to Public Relations Coordinator Nancy Lee, Exhibition Management Coordinator Carolyn Lifsey, and Director of Communications Lyn Winter.

Advice has come from many sources, but I would like to especially thank Hitoshi Abe, Donald Albrecht, Victoria Behner, Jean-Louis Cohen, Brooke Hodge, Ray Kappe, Qingyun Ma, and Andrew Zago, as well as the owners of the many homes we visited in preparing this exhibition. The clients who commissioned this outstanding architecture were incredibly generous in sharing their experiences. I would also like to thank all the firms and individuals from whom we requested pavilion designs for their hard work and ideas. All the designs are included herewith, although in the end we could only build a few. I thank Benjamin Ball and Gaston Nogues of Ball-Nogues Studio, Elena Manferdini, Marcelo Spina and Georgina Huljich of P-A-T-T-E-R-N-S, and Tom Wiscombe for offering wonderful glimpses into the near future of the profession of architecture.

I owe my sincerest thanks to my wife, Stephanie Emerson, not only for her unerring and patient spousal support but for her advice and expertise in the field of museums and particularly in the area of publishing. Finally, thanks go to my young son, Julian, whose sweet smile is the best part of the day.

Christopher Mount
Guest Curator, The Museum of Contemporary Art, Los Angeles

The Foundation of a New Sculpturalism
Christopher Mount

"It seems the culture of Los Angeles is in the process of being made, it is now L.A.'s time."

MICHAEL ROTONDI, 1987[1]

During the past quarter century, a significant proportion of the architecture produced in Los Angeles has been uniquely expressive, unnervingly experimental, and challenging. Unpredictably, these buildings and their architects have enjoyed substantial successes. There are architectural gems scattered throughout the city, hidden behind Victorian houses and popping up in industrial wastelands, barren suburbs, and the hills of tony neighborhoods. With a wonderful sense of democracy that is particular to Los Angeles, these structures admirably range in terms of program from the high to the low, from the grand concert hall to the gritty metal supplier's workshop. They are rebellious and avant-garde, even in an age when *avant-garde* may have little meaning, thanks to technology's swift dissemination of information and its immediate impact on design. Los Angeles architecture's defining elements often border on the "irrational and unstable," where dynamism is king, and it is as complex and diverse as the city from which it hails.

Although the rest of the world may have come late to the party, this architecture has been embraced internationally since the mid-1980s,

1. Michael Rotondi, quoted in Joseph Giovannini, "For a New Los Angeles Style, A Place in the Sun," *The New York Times*, April 16, 1987.

Eric Owen Moss Architects, Samitaur Tower, Culver City, California, 2010

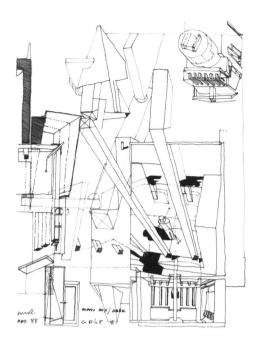

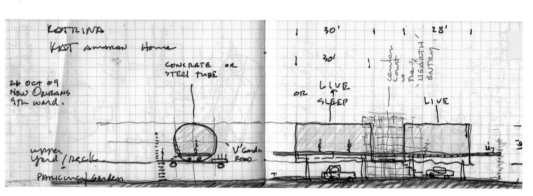

RoTo Architects, sketch for CDLT 1, 2,
Los Angeles, 1988

RoTo Architects, sketch for Katamaran
House, Ninth Ward, New Orleans, 2009

and its practitioners have been awarded two Pritzker Architecture Prizes, have been the subject of over one hundred published books (mostly monographs), have generated page upon page of editorial content, and have designed new buildings in every major city in the world, including destinations as diverse as China, Paris, Prague, Korea, Texas, Germany, and New York. Los Angeles has become an intellectual center for contemporary architecture, and its discourse is in part due to the vast local opportunities for architects in academia. Unique among major American cities, it maintains no fewer than five preeminent and/ or important architecture schools: University of California, Los Angeles (UCLA); Southern California Institute of Architecture (SCI-Arc); University of Southern California; Cal State Polytechnic University; and Woodbury University, in addition to a number of excellent art and design schools.

This exhibition identifies roughly three generations of practitioners who have made major contributions to the recent history of Los Angeles architecture, allowing for a healthy amount of dissimilarity among their approaches—the ways in which they work and, of course, their finished structures. There is "no single idea"[2] unifying these architects' work, as there was for the European modernists. Instead, this exhibition identifies a pluralism born out of an acceptance of ideas previously thought to be adversarial to the practice, including an embrace of ad-hocism, instability, and disjunction as well as a predilection for novelty. The work made in Los Angeles during the past twenty-five years represents not so much a rigid "school" but rather a free-floating "galaxy."[3] This convergence is not the

result of some secret pact, but of the location in which these architects have chosen to practice. Los Angeles is a sprawling city on the western edge of the United States, mythically regarded, for better or worse, as a sort of frontier town open to the new and certainly to those willing to reinvent. The city's history, economics, geography, and sociopolitics have influenced its architecture, and although many of these practitioners have gone on to build elsewhere, both nationally and internationally, their works are firmly rooted in Los Angeles' particular zeitgeist.

Action and making—instead of merely thinking and theorizing—have been paramount to the new spirit of design in Los Angeles, affording its architecture an uncommon avant-garde quality. At the same time, Los Angeles architects can be seen to share in a set of formal and theoretical values, most significantly an embrace of the intuitive, improvised, and synthetic. There is a delight in sabotage, in pushing the definitions of what architecture is, and subsequently boundaries are repeatedly broken through. A conscious disregard for corporate and traditional building methods has fomented a willingness to employ new forms and rethink even the basic elements of design. This approach has introduced new shapes[4] into the language of building, resulting in work that has often been called "willfully sculptural."

Ironically, architects rarely admit to being influenced by others' work unless, as Jeffrey Kipnis commented, "they are from a very distant land or have been dead for at least 200 years."[5] Demonstrating direct influences or clear dialectical progression in architecture is problematic

2. Thom Mayne, video interview with Charlie Rose, "An Hour with Architect Thom Mayne," December 2, 2005, available at http://www.charlierose.com/view/interview/636.

3. The idea of this group of architects forming a "galaxy" and not a school was first suggested to the author by the architectural historian Jean-Louis Cohen at an exhibition-planning meeting in New York on September 19, 2011.

4. See, for example, Frank O. Gehry's sliced cylinders, as seen at the Vitra Design Museum in Weil am Rhein, Germany, and many of his other works.
5. Jeffrey Kipnis, in a SCI-Arc lecture titled "Who Is Eric Moss?," March 6, 2012.

Oyler Wu Collaborative, *Centerstage*, installation at Graduation Pavilion, SCI-Arc, Los Angeles, 2012

because of the disconnection between ideas and actual built examples. The architects featured in this exhibition proudly think of themselves as a group of misfits or rabid individualists; however, they inhabit a city that has inspired, for whatever reason, unusually collegial relationships among them.[6] Of this group, Frank O. Gehry is the oldest and most established, and he is perhaps the most significant architect of the past half century. The extent of his influence on the others is open to debate; what Gehry and his "one-man revolution" may have caused most significantly is the opening of a Pandora's box of ideas that eventually forced the nurturing and acceptance of a broad range of astounding possibilities for what architecture could be.

This paradigmatic shift was intimately felt by a younger group that includes Thom Mayne, Michael Rotondi, Eric Owen Moss, Craig Hodgetts, Robert Mangurian, and the late Franklin D. Israel, with varying consequences. Mayne has referred to this unleashing of the potential of architecture as a kind of "infinite differentiation"[7]; for Moss the obligation of building became to challenge the viewer.[8] The (approximate) next generation, which includes Michael Maltzan, Neil M. Denari, Lorcan O'Herlihy, Greg Lynn, Barbara Bestor, Kevin Daly, and Michele Saee, learned well from that group but modified the lessons. Their exuberance and radicalism is more restrained, and their designs are seemingly more practical, with some elements of the modernist movement reasserted. Often more soothing and reassuring, their works may be shaped by a culmination of factors, including their "coming in at the end of a revolution,"[9] their makers' personal vision, and an increasingly contracting and conservative economy. Yet a quizzical nature is also expressed through an emphasis on unique forms, varying materials, vivid colors, and omnipresent invention. In many instances there is a unique informality to the architecture, which reflects its roots in Southern California.

The most recent generation of firms includes Ball-Nogues Studio, B + U, FreelandBuck, Predock Frane Architects, Atelier Manferdini, Tom Wiscombe Design, Oyler Wu Collaborative, and Layer, whose works are represented in this exhibition primarily by pavilions they have designed for installation in the museum. The technological advances initiated by Gehry and others led these practitioners to completely radical, increasingly digital ways of building and exploring form and

6. See the professional timeline in "Academic and Professional Timelines" on page 230–31 for more information about affiliations. **7.** Mayne, interview with the author, August 3, 2012.

Morphosis Architects, Landa Residence, Manhattan Beach, California, 1997

Morphosis Architects, in collaboration with printmakers Selwyn Ting and John Nichols, Sixth Street Composite Serigraph, 1988

Eric Owen Moss Architects, photomontage of Pterodactyl, Los Angeles, 2013

structure. For them, investigation is paramount, marking a shift in the way architectural practice has been understood. More openly theoretical and rooted in academia, this generation embraces a kind of structural sculpturalism that experiments with how buildings or installations might be made. Parametric studies and complex, non-euclidean geometries are tested in service of new construction materials and devices, brought both from the sophisticated aerospace industries and from the lowly world of detritus such as recycled paper. Interestingly, these firms' strong foundation in experimentation lends a circular aspect to the twenty-five-year span of this exhibition, as the earlier generation of Mayne, Gehry, Rotondi, Moss, and Hodgetts all began with small, investigative, workshoplike offices whose primary goal was reimagining the substance of architecture.

One of the most revolutionary aspects of this work is the primacy with which the strictly visual is pushed to the forefront, and this quality is the genesis for the exhibition and catalogue. This project is not a survey of what has been constructed since the mid-1980s or a list of "best works." Instead it is an attempt to tell the story of a significant period of architecture full of complexity and a form of building that delights in the abstract and flaunts a visual richness that seems contradictory to the sober times in which we live. Importantly, aside from the specially commissioned pavilion projects, all the work included in the exhibition is either built or in the process of being built, the fact of which adds a quality of authority to its radicalism. This is architecture that wows by boldly challenging the status quo.

The Emergence of Sculpturalism

Sculpture or *sculptural* are often considered dirty words in architecture because they imply impracticality. This attitude is to a large degree an emotional vestige of modernism, a movement that frowned on the excessive or decorative as wasteful and unnecessary. European high modernists of the 1920s and 30s were so firmly rooted in the admiration of mass production and the possibilities that the Industrial Revolution afforded that they clung to the idea that multiplicity and large-scale production were the ingredients for a better way of life for all. Systems and a priori ideas of rationalism dominated, and with few exceptions artistic individualism or personalization were repressed. In part, the concept of sculpturalism reflects a philosophy of building, a matured liberalism that is slightly wary of utopian causes and collective activities and instead keen for the reassertion of individualism. In the broadest sense, this is a search for a greater democratization, humanity, and ultimately architecture that better reflects our times. Ignored are the modernist dicta of "less is more," "form follows function," and "truth in materials" taught to previous generations. As Gehry wrote, "I am a strict modernist in the sense of believing in purity, that you shouldn't decorate. And yet buildings need decoration, because they need scaling elements. They need to be human scale, in my opinion. They can't just be faceless things. That's how some modernism failed. When it started to be used by developers, it became faceless. It became a language that self-destructed. What was missing was human scale."[10] His statement is reminiscent of a wonderful quote by the Finnish architect Alvar Aalto, an influence on Gehry who, reacting to the totalitarian subtext of German modernism, wrote, "I cannot get my needs into order,

8. See Eric Owen Moss and Brad Collins, *Eric Owen Moss: Buildings and Projects* (New York: Rizzoli, 1991).

9. Moss used this term in his introduction to a lecture by Michael Maltzan at SCI-Arc on September 27, 2006.

10. Mildred Friedman, *Gehry Talks: Architecture + Process* (New York: Universe, 2002), 47–48.

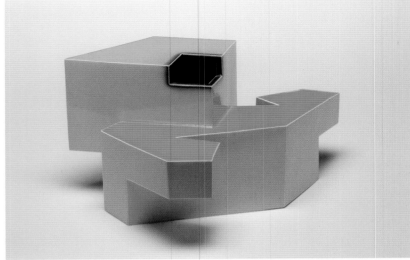

Edward Kienholz, *The Wait*, 1964–65
Wood, fabric, polyester resin, flock, metal, bones,
glass, paper, leather, varnish, gelatin-silver prints,
taxidermied cat, live parakeet, wicker, and plastic,
80 x 160 x 84 inches, Whitney Museum of American
Art, New York, gift of the Howard and Jean Lipman
Foundation, Inc., photo by Sheldan C. Collins, ©
Kienholz, courtesy L.A. Louver, Venice, California

Ken Price, *Hawaiian*, 1980
Ceramic, 5 5/8 x 11 1/2 x 9 1/2 inches, Betty Lee and
Aaron Stern Collection, courtesy of Ken Price Studio,
photo © Fredrik Nilsen

so how can I live in a purely functionalist house."[11] High modernism fell short in its connection with man's imperfections, and these new buildings represent a personal liberation more sympathetic with an American ideal of democracy and personal expression. As Rotondi has pointed out, "The fragmentation that exists everywhere in society is one of the issues that interests us in architecture."[12]

In the visual arts, the definition of the term *sculpture* has exploded since the late 1960s, used to refer to Earthworks, Minimalism, performances, environments, installations, and three-dimensional collages as well as more traditional sculpted forms.[13] *Sculptural* is applied in this instance as a way of expanding the nomenclature of architecture; it signals an opening up of possibilities, nodding to the diversity that has been successfully promulgated by recent generations of Los Angeles practitioners. If, in recent memory, the fine arts have encroached on architectural practice and the exploration of space, then is not the reverse fair as well? The projects featured in this exhibition are highly functional—nowadays they must be in order to be built—and even frequently utilize sophisticated technologies to lessen their environmental impact, but they are also formally expressive and visually rich. They share a playful multiplicity of interconnecting pieces and forms. Folding roofs, acute angles, unusual corners, and eccentric relationships between the most mundane of architectural features (from floors to walls to ceilings) are prevalent, as are dramatic shifts in volume and voids pierced through walls and facades. This architecture is more about the uneasy conglomeration than the fused whole.[14] The result can be both

stirring and unsettling—a sort of huge assemblage manufactured from contrasting materials with an artistic complexity more in tune with the experience of sculpture than what we have come to expect from many years of orderly and purportedly functional architecture.

A profound interest in the unpredictable, unfinished, and the seemingly random is prevalent in Los Angeles. For some architects these qualities reflect the general state of society and the condition of life in the early twenty-first century. These are, however, quite radical ideas when applied to the very necessary static nature of architecture. Can the conservative eyes with which we insist on seeing architecture accept these ideas? And how is the temporal introduced in a structure that is intended to last for many years? Shifting facades and cantilevered elements that appear without a purpose suggest a quality of something unresolved and still in transformation. Overwhelmingly self-confident and frequently oozing with personal expression, the buildings belie a strong sense of the auteur. All these successful firms have created for themselves definitive styles and signature geometric vocabularies more common to the small workshop than the large global offices many have become. They remain—despite much success—attached to personal and investigative practices. In opposition to much of what the modernist movement was about, in its search for the "objective" solution, this architecture deliberately and unabashedly embraces its "subjectiveness." This is perhaps more aligned with what we can expect from visual artists than an overarching rational authoritarian ideal of how we should live.

11. Alvar Aalto, in a speech given in London, 1957.

12. Rotondi, quoted in Joseph Giovannini, "The Limit of Chaos Tempts a New School of Architects," *The New York Times*, February 4, 1988.

13. See Rosalind Krauss, "Sculpture in the Expanded Field," *October* 8 (Spring 1979): 30–44.
14. Kipnis lecture, 2012.

From left: Frederick Fisher, Robert Mangurian
Eric Owen Moss, Coy Howard, Craig
Hodgetts, Thom Mayne, and Frank Gehry,

Santa Monica, California, 1980
photo © Ave Pildas

Franklin D. Israel Design Associates,
Drager House, Berkeley, California, 1994

A more immediate reason for connecting the term *sculptural* to architecture is the influence, whether direct or through osmosis, of Los Angeles' vibrant art scene of the 1960s and 70s on the city's architecture, and in particular, its dominant embrace of sculpture. The first iterations of Los Angeles' architectural sculpturalism appeared in the mid-1970s in the rough-hewn and funky "slum by the sea" of Venice Beach and neighboring Santa Monica, partially as a result of the architects and artists living near one another in those areas. Architects Mayne, Gehry, Hodgetts, and Coy Howard as well as influential artists Billy Al Bengston, Ed Moses, Ken Price, Larry Bell, and Edward Kienholz enjoyed the affordable rents and proximity to the beach. Much of this architecture was, like the fine art, provisional in nature, made from what was on hand, born out of a kind of *arte povera*. Englishman Charles Jencks, a professor at UCLA, first codified an idea of the LA School in a 1983 exhibition titled "Los Angeles Now," further developing the idea in his 1993 book *Heteropolis: Los Angeles, the Riots and the Strange Beauty of Hetero-Architecture*. In it, he differentiates Los Angeles architecture of this period from postmodernist design: "Frank Gehry, Morphosis, Eric Owen Moss, Frank Israel and a host of other designers have begun to fashion a hetero-architecture which suggests ethnic pluralism without naming it, and includes various tastes-cultures without piling on Corinthian columns and Latino quotations."[15] He further asserts, "The L.A. School was, and remains a group of individualized mavericks, more at home together in an exhibition than in each other's homes. There is also a particular self-image involved in this Non-School, which exacerbates the situation. All of its members see themselves as outsiders, on the margins

challenging the establishment with an informal and demanding architecture; one that must be carefully read."[16]

Other monikers for this early group include the Gehry School, the Gehry Kids, and the Gehry Schule. Olivier Boissière's 1980 *Domus* article "The Young Architects of California" contains one of the earliest acknowledgments of the emergence of this group. He wrote, "At present there exists something of a group, people who have no formal ties and who know, appreciate and are ready to help one another if need be and whose friendship is all the more untroubled for the fact that their researches move in clearly different directions.... What these young Californians have in common is the place they work in California that puts up the least resistance to innovation and adventure."[17] In a thoughtful 1995 essay for *Progressive Architecture*, John Morris Dixon referred to this generation as the Santa Monica School because of their concentration on Los Angeles' Westside. He viewed them as "bohemians" building unusual dwellings for artists, art dealers, and college professors (in other words, the intelligentsia). Describing their work as "architecture as art for the low-budget collector," he went on to write, "like the arugula and sashimi that were becoming appreciated in the same circles, this edgy, iconoclastic architecture was definitely an acquired taste."[18]

Further defining and bringing attention to what was occurring in Los Angeles, *Experimental Architecture in Los Angeles* was published in 1992 with essays by Gehry, Aaron Betsky, John Chase, and Leon Whiteson. Chase addressed a key formalist element of Los Angeles

15. Charles Jencks, *Heteropolis: Los Angeles, the Riots and the Strange Beauty of Hetero-Architecture* (New York: St. Martin's Press, 1993), 15.

16. Ibid., 34.
17. Olivier Boissière, "The Young Architects of California," *Domus*, no. 604 (March 1980): 20–21.

18. John Morris Dixon, "The Santa Monica School: What's Its Lasting Contribution?," *Progressive Architecture* 76, no. 5 (March 1995): 64.

**Grinstein/Daniels Architects,
Kentucky Fried Chicken Restaurant,
Los Angeles, 1990**

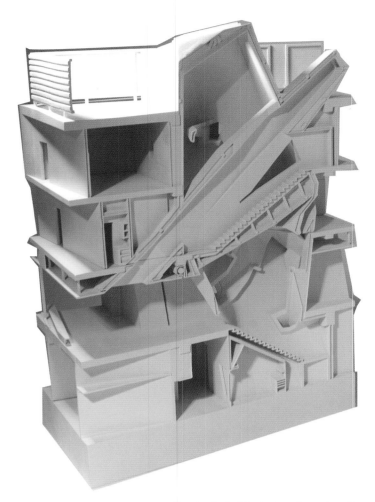

**Morphosis Architects, two views of section
model of stairway for Cahill Center for Astronomy
and Astrophysics at Caltech, Pasadena,
California, 2008**

architecture: "Casual composition increases the sense of fragmentation and motion in work. Such buildings suggest that they could just as
easily have been put together in several other ways. They imply that they
are the record of a process more than they are the embodiment of a
final product." He continued, "The use of fragmented forms in so many
of the projects may also reflect the architect's desire to avoid making
completely comprehensible forms reflecting the state of flux of a shifting
and transitory society."[19] Enthusiastic acceptance soon comes in 1996
with much praise from the *New York Times* architecture critic Herbert
Muschamp, who wrote a warning for the rest of the profession in
America: "Architecture, at least from a New Yorker's point of view, is the
art that got away, the art that went west because it needed more room
to breathe. In the last decades, Los Angeles has eclipsed New York as
the country's leading city for contemporary architecture."[20]

The initial generation practicing between the late 1980s and today—
Gehry, Mayne, Rotondi, Hodgetts + Fung, and Moss—flirted early in
their careers with historical postmodernism. Many came to professional
maturity when postmodernism was embraced as a kind of solution and
exit path to the rut that modernism had become, both from a stylistic
and theoretical standpoint. Looking for a broader vocabulary and
something that might allow for a greater personal expression in addition
to a more "humane" kind of building, this was a possible path forward.
Although their work never reaches the zenith of historical appropriation
of, say, the buildings of Michael Graves, there is a theoretical basis
that attaches them to the writings and work of Robert Venturi and

Denise Scott Brown, especially Venturi's introduction to *Complexity and
Contradiction in Architecture*, which develops a basic groundwork for
much of what has occurred in Los Angeles:

> I like complexity and contradiction in architecture....I speak of a
> complex and contradictory architecture based on the richness
> and ambiguity of modern experience, including that experience
> which is inherent in art....I aim for vitality as well as validity....
> I like elements which are hybrid rather than "pure," compromis-
> ing rather than "clean," distorted rather than straightforward,
> ambiguous rather than "articulated," perverse as well as

19. John Chase, "Modernism and the Los Angeles Vernacular,"
in *Experimental Architecture in Los Angeles* (New York: Rizzoli,
1992), 136.

20. Herbert Muschamp, "A City Poised on Glitter and Ashes,"
The New York Times, March 10, 1996.

RoTo Architects, living room of Carlson-
Reges House, Los Angeles, 1996

Saee Studio, drawing for 434 Apartments,
Los Angeles, 1989

impersonal, boring as well as "interesting," conventional
rather than "designed," accommodating rather than excluding,
redundant rather than simple, vestigial as well as innovating,
inconsistent and equivocal rather than direct and clear. I am
for messy vitality over obvious unity. I include the non-sequitur
and proclaim the duality....I am for richness of meaning rather
than clarity of meaning; for the implicit function as well as the
explicit function....A valid architecture evokes many levels of
meaning and combinations of focus: its space and its elements
become readable and workable in several ways at once....It
must embody the difficult unity of inclusion rather than the easy
unity of exclusion....More is not less.[21]

What is interesting is how the architects included in this exhibition have
followed this call for complexity not with the historical appropriation that
many, including Venturi himself, implemented, but instead have looked
to the history of modernism for inspiration, rearranging the materials so
important to modernists—glass, steel, brick, concrete, and wood—into
a current kind of bricolage architecture. As Dixon wrote, "At a time when
postmodernism was offering up nostalgia tinged with irony, the Santa
Monica group started with the premise that the present was okay."[22]
Instead of appropriation and historical revivalism, these architects
reinvestigated the stuff of architecture, the two-by-fours, steel beams,
joints, and mutation of materials into here to unknown shape and forms,
reinventing in the present.

Sculpturalism and the City

During the 1970s and early 80s, some Los Angeles architects often
spoke of feeling isolated from developments on the East Coast and in
Europe. In some ways, they benefited from this condition, as they were
distant from the corporate power base lauded over by Philip Johnson
and the Museum of Modern Art as well as the very successful and
relatively conservative practitioners I. M. Pei; Skidmore, Owings and
Merrill; Edward Larrabee Barnes; Charles Gwathmey; and Richard Meier.
Thus, as Michele Saee described, the architecture studio in Los Angeles
was "a less formal place" where "playing" was a crucial aspect of the
creative process.[23] Rotondi has observed, "The work appears fresh
because it is from this place, not another—the buildings don't derive
from Europe, like those on the East Coast" and "the umbilical cord never
made it across the Rockies from Europe."[24] Southern California architects were able to invent, research, and rethink without the distraction
of an aggressive press or dismissive competitors. As Gehry recognized,
"There has always been a freedom out here that lets us grow our own
ideas and get them built."[25]

Los Angeles has been much romanticized as a city embodying an
American ideal of freedom only found at the periphery, outside the
mainstream. Although no longer the tabula rasa it was during the 1920s
when its first housing boom began, Los Angeles is still a very new
metropolis full of distinct experiences and identities only a short car
ride away from each other. With little vernacular tradition aside from
the Spanish influence, the urban landscape freed architects from the

21. Robert Venturi, *Complexity and Contradiction in Architecture*
(New York: Museum of Modern Art, 2002), 16.
22. Dixon, "The Santa Monica School," 64.

23. Michele Saee, conversation with the author, June 14, 2012.
24. Rotondi, quoted in Giovannini, "For A New Los Angeles Style,
A Place in the Sun."

25. Gehry, "Gehry and the Los Angeles Scene," public discussion
at the Getty Center, December 13, 2011.

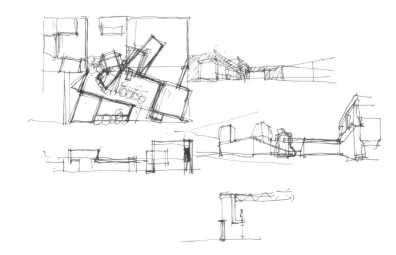

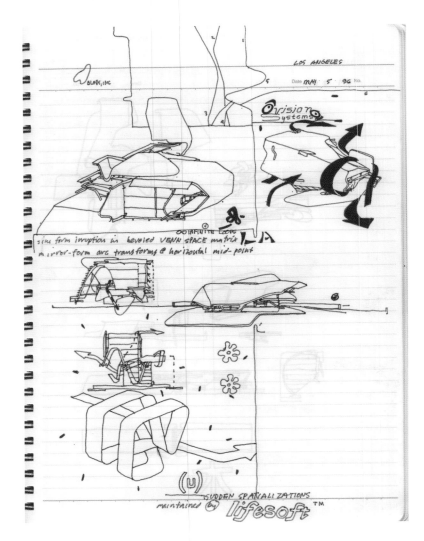

Above: Michael Maltzan Architecture, sketch for Inner-City Arts, Los Angeles, 2008   **Right: Neil M. Denari Architects, untitled sketch, 1996**

necessity of strict contextualization and its ordained rooflines, step-back rules, cornices, and use of traditional materials such as brick or stone, as in older, more densely populated cities. Los Angeles' architecture is unburdened, able to stand assertively against a backdrop frequently made up of parking lots and mini-malls. Traditional building types, common in much of the rest of the world, have had less of a stranglehold on the creative imagination, resulting in a variety of forms that lack historical precedent. These structures have an unnerving, anonymous quality devoid of any kind of semiotic indication of function. Because they are often at the precipice of actually reimagining a basic form or type of architecture—house, store, post office, library, museum, or office building—they exude few of the vernacular signs that we have come to expect. As Herbert Muschamp so nicely wrote about Moss's work, "He teaches old buildings new skills."[26]

Compared to other cultural capitals, Los Angeles is a more affordable place to live as well as to build. Throughout the twentieth century, Los Angeles grew across a wide swath of land as a result of real estate developers' insistence on the superiority of the single-family home.[27] The city's public sphere has regularly been subjugated to the private. As Hitoshi Abe, chair of the architecture department at UCLA, has written, "Experimentation emerges from the city as a site of extreme individualism. In this sense, experimentation in Los Angeles is about self-reflection and independent individuals striving to extend their own capabilities and the limits of possibilities."[28] A majority of the firms included in this exhibition got their start designing small private homes,

and in fact the most inventive architecture still occurs in the private realm, a condition that would be unusual in most American cities. That so much of this architecture is hidden like small treasures, available to only the home owner and invited guests, has only encouraged a kind of boldness on behalf of the designer and the clients.

The recent history of Los Angeles' development has involved the reclamation of industrial areas or areas at the edge, downtown, Culver City, and even to some degree Venice, often for economic reasons. An "economy of means" is a theme that is central to the history of Southern California architecture. One of the most common projects has been the addition to or renovation of an existing space, one of the most famous being Gehry's add-on to his Santa Monica home, begun in 1977 and remodeled again between 1991 and 1994. But there are

26. Muschamp, "Architecture View: An Enterprise Zone for the Imagination," *The New York Times*, March 14, 1993.

27. Chase, "Modernism and the Los Angeles Vernacular," 134.
28. Hitoshi Abe, "The New Ecologies in Los Angeles—Design and Technology," *A + U* (August 2008): 10.

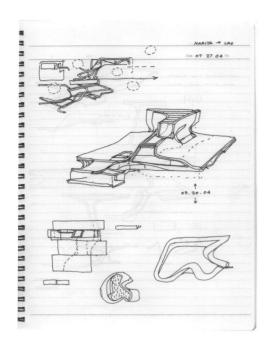

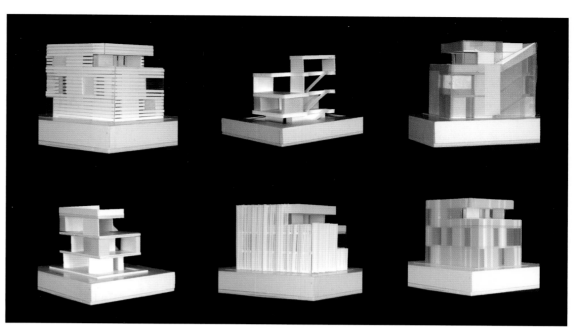

Neil M. Denari Architects, untitled sketch,
2004

XTEN Architecture, process models of
Surfhouse, Hermosa Beach, California, 2007

many other examples, including early renovations to homes in Venice by Morphosis, many of Israel's innovative homes, and more recently, Daly Genik Architects' Winnett (2007) and XTEN Architecture's glamorous Nakahouse (2010) in the Hollywood Hills. Hodgetts + Fung's Towell Library (1992) for UCLA, built as temporary storage and library space while the permanent library was being upgraded, is a remarkable piece of affordable ad-hocism at an institutional level. On a larger scale, Daly Genik has remodeled mini-mall buildings into a colorful middle school for Camino Nuevo Charter Academy (2000); Maltzan renovated an old auto-body shop to build Inner-City Arts (2008); and Gehry transformed a former police-car garage into the Temporary Contemporary, now the Geffen Contemporary at MOCA (1983). These buildings are hybrids—a kind of architectural assemblage; they require a willingness to adapt and a sensitivity to cost more than is typically necessary for ground-up projects. Mirroring very much the spirit of Los Angeles, they are about the reinvention of the old into the new.

In Los Angeles, a building can resemble a freestanding object, with the city offering multiple points from which to see it, whether approaching by car or walking around it. The general lack of verticality in most cases only enhances this. A bright "safety orange" house, a shining metal-clad concert hall, a science building whose facade seems to be separating from the overall structure: these are not works attempting to fit in. Rather, they embrace Mayne's notion that "neutrality is failure."[29] A good deal of the city's common commercial architecture suffers from a mediocrity and a certain dystopic aura. Stand on any main intersection

(for instance, La Brea Avenue and Santa Monica Boulevard) and witness the plethora of visual clutter—pedestrians, street lamps, signs, cars four lanes deep, more signage, a parking lot, a glass facade with more signs. Where is the architecture but buried in the recesses, anonymous? One must wonder whether the assertiveness of much of this work suggests a reaction to this recessing/retardation of the importance of the actual building. Some of the designers, Moss and Mayne in particular, seem to embrace the dystopic in their buildings, albeit in a much more artful manner. Their extruding forms—perforated windows and twisted members—suggest the collision and conflict the designers believe is so prevalent in civilization today. Their assertiveness results in a kind of politicization of architecture, one that mirrors the current discordant state of society.

On the other hand, the prevalence of sunlight and the mild climate have enlivened Los Angeles architecture and have been a major factor in its sculptural and investigative elements. As Coy Howard remarked, "you didn't really have to be that knowledgeable about building,"[30] because structural problems such as leaks or gaps could be fixed on the fly. Stone, steel, and cement are cast aside in favor of exuberant and joyful facades; bright reds, oranges, yellows, and pale greens and blues create refreshing palettes that differ from those used elsewhere. Lorcan O'Herlihy Architects' Formosa 1140 (2008), Neil M. Denari Architects' Alan-Voo House (2007), Daly Genik Architects' Winnett, and Michael Maltzan Architects' Rainbow Apartments (2006) and One Santa Fe mixed-use project (to be completed in 2014) each feature vibrant

29. Mayne, interview with Rose, 2005.

30. Coy Howard, conversation with the author, July 27, 2012.

**Gehry Partners, Beekman Tower,
New York, 2011**

Larry Bell, *Untitled*, 1968
Grey and clear glass panels, 10 panels: 96 x 72 x ³/₈
inches each, courtesy of the artist, installation in

"14 Sculptors: The Industrial Edge," Walker Art
Center, Minneapolis, 1969

exteriors that enhance their abstract formal qualities. Such vibrant coloration has also created clearer delineations between forward and recessed spaces, as can be seen in a number of Maltzan's projects. The differentiation of color is a device that is frequently used to emphasize the pronounced and intentional abstraction of volumes.

It would be an oversight to discuss Los Angeles architecture without acknowledging the influence of the entertainment industry. The spirit of Hollywood is deeply intertwined with the city's art and design worlds. Comfortable in the idea of making and remaking itself, Los Angeles does so architecturally at a quick pace. Artificiality and questions around the social construction of reality are everyday concerns, whether emanating from the fake facades of movie lots or the fairy-tale cottages built by Disney set designers in Los Feliz. Even its basic urban fabric—with a central cement-lined "river" and a "lake," in Silver Lake, that is actually a reservoir—seems unduly man-made. Contrary to having a negative effect on architecture, this casual flirtation with artificiality has encouraged remarkable experimentation. The persistent question of the fragility of reality is just beneath the surface in much of this work, particularly in some of the more extravagant projects. As Chase has written, "This architecture draws on research by artists into the relationship between artifice and experience or which transforms itself into set design at an urban scale."[31]

Sculpturalism and Technology

Significant reasons for the greater sculptural exuberance of this architecture reside in the way it is conceived. In Los Angeles, an adaptability and capacity for improvisation is afforded even late in the process, on site. This is made possible by the prevalent use of low-cost wood construction, which allows for a certain amount of on-site changes and informal decisions. Ann Bergren recalls that her house, designed by Morphosis between 1982 and 1986, was very much improvised on site, with few existing drawings and only a study model hauled to and from the location.[32] There is of course the archetypal example of Gehry's Santa Monica home, a kind of full-size experimental model. The Carlson-Reges House (1996), located next to a train depot and designed by Rotondi, utilized scrap iron from the owner's metal salvage business including a sliced/halved oil tank that on the owners' insistence became a cantilevered swimming pool projected over the industrial surroundings. As Jencks explains, "ubiquitous deconstruction and reconstruction" has become an "architectural language."[33]

Architects on the West Coast were some of the first in the world to sincerely embrace the "sketch model"[34] as an initial device for investigation of form. No firm's design process is exactly the same; however, the introduction of modeling in three dimensions has for the most part been applied sooner in the process and more vigorously in California. Gehry is of course most well known for sculpting his work out of various materials by hand as seen so vividly in Sydney Pollack's film *Sketches of Frank Gehry* (2005). With the recent availability of smaller three-dimensional

31. Chase, "Modernism and the Los Angeles Vernacular," 132.

32. Ann Bergren, conversation with the author, July 10, 2012.
33. Jencks, *Heteropolis*, 15.

34. This term has come to mean a three-dimensional model that complements or replaces the initial or early exploration that used to take place in the sketch (pencil on paper) form.

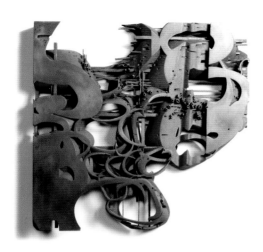

**Morphosis Architects, "drawdle" of
LIUFFAIO, 2011**

**Rudolph Schindler, Adolph Tischler
Residence, Los Angeles, 1950**

printing and milling, the shift to small developmental models and away from drawing on computer (or paper) has been a prominent tool for firms and architects as diverse as Morphosis, Moss, Maltzan, Saee, Lynn, and Hagy Belzberg. What this shift affords is a more complete and better understanding of complex three-dimensional relationships and an inherent ease with which to mutate, collapse, or bend forms.

Los Angeles architects have frequently been lauded for their early utilization of computer software. Gehry's use of the aerospace software CATIA (Computer Aided Three-Dimensional Interactive Application) revolutionized how structures are built, a revolution that continues in the work of younger generations. This software has not been used to make rational, orderly, Miesian architecture, but rather as a tool to sculpt and mold forms. Ironically, all this sophisticated technology has been utilized to reintroduce a sense of the hand, or craftsmanship, into architecture. Gehry Partners' Beekman Tower (2011) in New York features an undulating facade that suggests a sculptor working in clay with a ribbon tool. Its "originality" or "authenticity"[35] comes via machinery, hard drives, wires, and blips and bleeps—technology that is able to take the spirit and style of, say, a small tabletop ceramic and increase its scale thousands of times over.[36] Astonishingly this architecture does not require repetition and easily multiplied pieces such as are prevalent in ordinary glass skyscrapers. Instead, it is "fractal"[37] in nature and the possibilities for "differentiation" are immense when the computer and cost of actual production is only marginally more than the ordinary straightforward concrete, glass, or steel building.

Sculpturalism and Art

Out of the ashes of postmodern architecture and its inherent push for greater pluralism and complexity, many Los Angeles architects, Gehry in particular, chose to absorb lessons from the visual arts. This curiosity about the fine arts, specifically local sculpture, ultimately became part of the formal and theoretical foundation for all the architecture on view in this exhibition. Gehry has long embraced his connection to the artistic bohemia of Los Angeles' Westside, recalling, "From the beginning of my adult life I have always related better to artists than to architects,"[38] claiming, "I have lived a double life."[39] Architecture during the 1960s was dominated by the politically progressive modernists Gregory Ain, Pierre Koenig, A. Quincy Jones, Raphael Soriano, and Craig Ellwood, who advocated for what some of the next generation perceived as a rigid and limited view of how the profession should proceed. For Hodgetts, Gehry, Mayne, and others, the influence of the visual arts made them aware of the liberated feeling of actually "making stuff."

Since World War II, some of the most successful and inventive design to come from California has had very modest beginnings and was essentially "made in the garage." Second World War veterans built elaborate and colorful hot rods; Hewlett-Packard and Apple developed computers; and early surfboards, snowboards, and even the plywood Eames chair all started in this fashion. The joy of tinkering and the resulting hands-on quality is not irrelevant to the genesis of much of this work. From the early firms and architects—Rotondi, Mangurian, Israel, and others—to the very contemporary installations of Ball-Nogues Studio, Atelier Elena

35. This is Mayne's phrase.

36. In addition, this technology also makes the complex functional program possible.
37. See Jencks, *The New Paradigm in Architecture: The Language of Postmodernism* (New Haven, Conn.: Yale University Press, 2002).

38. Gehry lecture, 2011.
39. Ibid.

**Armet Davis Newlove Architects,
Pann's Restaurant, Los Angeles, 1958**
Photo © Jack Laxer, Pacific Palisades,
California

Manferdini, and Oyler Wu Collaborative, there is a strong tradition and interest in architecture as craft and the ingenuity that can result. Much is made by hand, all in a less formal environment. Even the sophisticated digital explorations of Greg Lynn developed via complex software quickly become physical handheld forms in his studio.

Since the 1960s, a broad variety of art has wielded an influence on Los Angeles architecture. There was large-scale work naturally sympathetic to it, including most obviously the dissected houses of Gordon Matta-Clark, the steel monoliths of Richard Serra, and Earthworks and Light and Space work by Michael Heizer, James Turrell, and Robert Irwin. On a smaller scale, the work of Los Angeles–based ceramists Ken Price (a close friend of Gehry's) and Peter Voulkos and sculptor Larry Bell had substantial effect, as did the various constructions and paintings by local artists such as Ed Moses, Billy Al Bengston, Peter Alexander, and

Chuck Arnoldi. Perhaps there is in the work of Moss, Gehry, and even some of the younger generation of Patrick Tighe and Lynn a "preference for the part over the whole."[40] Richard Weinstein addressed this relationship between architecture and sculpture: "In this reality, pieces of buildings become sculpture, detach themselves from the frame to seek daylight and assert their presence as carriers of the works' concentrated emotions. Today the distinction between architecture and sculpture is often ambiguous and the criteria that help us to understand each are difficult to find."[41] Gehry has said that the sails of a ship were his inspiration for both the Walt Disney Concert Hall (2003) and the IAC Headquarters (2007). Moss's Pterodactyl (1999), Stealth (2002), and Samitaur Tower (2010) are futuristic structures that cunningly represent clever and effective promotion for the clients' companies.

In the early 1980s and 90s, the almost-collaged buildings of Morphosis, Gehry, Hodgetts, and Mangurian and Howard owed a debt to California assemblage artists including Kienholz, Betye Saar, Bruce Conner, and George Herms.[42] These architects borrowed assemblage artists' egalitarian spirit and use of a variety of materials. At the same time, the profession of architecture had been years removed from any embrace of the handcrafted, favoring a more cerebral kind of practice. More acute for these architects was an understanding of how disorder and chaos can be turned into a pleasing and compelling object (building) and a faith in their possibilities. Drawn to the informal crafted quality of assemblage work, architects were also fascinated by its repurposing of everyday urban detritus. Assemblage became a powerful metaphor for a

40. Kipnis lecture, 2012.

41. Richard Weinstein, *Morphosis, Volume 2: Buildings and Projects, 1989–1992* (New York: Rizzoli, 1999), 16.

42. These artists were followed by a subsequent influential generation that included Nancy Rubins, Michael C. McMillen, Mike Kelley, and, to some degree, Chris Burden.

Ball-Nogues Studio, closed (opposite right) and open (above) views of *YEVRUS 1, Negative Impression*, SCI-Arc, Los Angeles, 2012

Israel, Callas, Shortridge Design Associates, Fine Arts Building, University of California, Riverside, 2001

new method of practice, and it very conveniently seemed to complement the overall urban fabric of Los Angeles. As a formal device, it enhances the fractal quality of the architecture and the assertiveness of the pieces as not part of a unified whole.

Precursors and Postscript

This essay is not intended to give a complete historical preface of sculpturalism's influences; however, there are a number of formal and theoretical precursors worth examining, if only briefly. The small, experimental studio that Rudolph Schindler began in the early 1920s was a significant precedent.[43] Schindler's house on Kings Road, which he and his family shared briefly with Richard Neutra and his wife, is a kind of full-scale material experiment, with concrete pillars buried in the ground with wood posts and lintels and interceding spaces separated by glass or semitransparent canvas panels. Like the contemporary California architects, Schindler was enamored with the possibilities the warm weather afforded for new kinds of living spaces. A verticality and geometric playfulness,[44] often present in the shifting planes, runs throughout his work, and more formal connections can be seen in the geometrics of the later Kallis and Tischler residences.

Other local historical precedents are numerous, from the high to low, including the Case Study House program's pursuit of affordability and its fly-by-the-seat-of-your-pants construction; the wonderfully sculptural and idiosyncratic works of John Lautner; and the expressive, geometric play of Lloyd Wright as well as that of his father, Frank Lloyd Wright.

An "adoration of the joint" and obsession with detailing and the hand-crafted has precedent in the ornate Arts and Crafts work of the brothers Greene & Greene. And many of these architects have been influenced by vernacular forms that delight in the theatrical, like the folded sloping rooflines of Armet and Davis's Googie architecture. There is of course the prominent shadow of Simon Rodia, an outsider who tirelessly constructed Watts Towers with discarded debris and found materials, an isolated loner whose singular vision experiments resulted in the remarkable structure that is one of the city's best-known and loved monuments.

The architects included in this exhibition share a general openness and egalitarian nature, and they have charmingly absorbed many influences without the preordained judgmental approach typical of those devoted to earlier modernist theories. For the newer firms, all these far-reaching developments of the past two generations have become normalized, and the vocabulary of a free expression becomes a tool or a second-hand language to apply at will. Unfortunately, for this generation there has been less building opportunity thanks to both a terrible recession and the uncertainty brought on by the terrorist attacks of 2001 and the subsequent foreign wars. Additionally, it can take years of toil before architects receive extensive commissions. Many of these practitioners have turned to academia and explored architecture via installations and smaller-scale projects. Firms such as Ball-Nogues Studio and designers including Elena Manferdini, Florencia Pita, Tom Wiscombe, and Jason Payne have embraced the theme of investigation that began more than twenty-five years ago on the Westside but also view the practice of

43. The influence of Viennese postwar architecture, including the work of Wolf Prix and Coop Himmelb(l)au, Hans Hollein, and others on California architecture and this group of architects is immense and a worthy topic for another essay or publication.

44. This emphasis on the relationship between rectangles echoes the European modernism of the De Stijl movement.

**Patrick Tighe Architecture, rendering of
Karp Residence, Los Angeles, 2014 (projected completion)**

architecture in a broader manner. The sculpturalism becomes a vocabulary or a palette from which to work. Instead of the "stuff of building," such as exposed bolts, nails, plasterboard, or two-by-fours, these firms have opted for a digital silkiness clearly not made by hand. It suggests that this period the exhibition covers could be summarized as a first embrace of the handmade and heteromorphic transformed by software toward a more unified and digital-morphic style.

It is truly remarkable to consider this work from the perspective of roughly forty years ago[45]—not just the most radical of Gehry, Morphosis, or Moss, but also more modest projects such as VOID's Bobco Metals Co. (2004), XTEN Architecture's Nakahouse, Tighe's Gelner Residence (2010), Denari's L.A. Eyeworks (2002), or O'Herlihy's Formosa 1140. These are projects that diverge completely from the path that was prescribed for an American profession enthralled with the historicism of postmodernism or the cool somberness of the "New York Whites."[46] It is as if architecture had to be lifted and taken somewhere else, across the country, as if some mad Hollywood science-fiction director got hold of the whole profession and taught it another way to build and, fundamentally, to see architecture. In the end, all this work has created a new perspective from which to speak of democracy and architecture. It has become a wonderfully transformative and healthy period for the profession, which has sought to put humanism in its many guises back in the art form. Gone are the old-fashioned leftist ideals of communal experience valued by the European modernists and their rigid formulaic solutions. Instead, like any good Western pioneer, these architects have

reasserted the individual and his or her freedoms (particularly in terms of expression) at the forefront of the profession, bringing architecture back from the doldrums of the early 1970s. Visual delight and its perfect partners—puzzlement and intellectual inquisition—have joined once again. Most significantly these architects have proven that the profession can still be inventive, that dynamism and freedom from convention can be positive, that diverse forms and textures express the pluralism of our society and liberate us from hierarchy. As Dixon concludes in his defining Santa Monica School article, "Working in a period of doubt and nostalgia these architects have encouraged all of us—architects, critics and public—to ponder the potential of innovative form-making, to enrich our lives."[47]

45. Philip Johnson makes a similar statement in an interview in the film *Sketches of Frank Gehry* by Sydney Pollack, 2005.

46. Unfortunately there is not room here to discuss the late postmodernist works of James Wines and SITE's Best Product Company showrooms, whose disintegrating and collapsing facades may be the most accurate progenitor of some of this California work.

47. Dixon, "The Santa Monica School," 64.

FRANK O. GEHRY & ASSOCIATES / GEHRY PARTNERS

Frank O. Gehry & Associates, Team Disneyland Administration Building,
Anaheim, California, 1995

Frank O. Gehry & Associates, Frederick R. Weisman Art and Teaching Museum, University of Minnesota, Minneapolis, 1993

Frank O. Gehry & Associates, Vitra Design Museum, Weil am Rhein, Germany, 1989

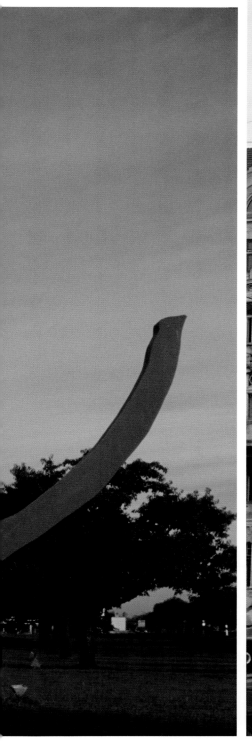

Frank O. Gehry & Associates, Nationale-Nederlanden Building, Prague, in collaboration with Studio V. H., 1996

FRANK O. GEHRY & ASSOCIATES / GEHRY PARTNERS

Frank O. Gehry & Associates, Der Neue Zollhof, Düsseldorf, 1999

Frank O. Gehry & Associates, Experience Music Project, Seattle, 2000

FRANK O. GEHRY & ASSOCIATES / GEHRY PARTNERS

Gehry Partners, Ray and Maria Stata Center, Massachusetts Institute of Technology, Cambridge, Massachusetts, 2004

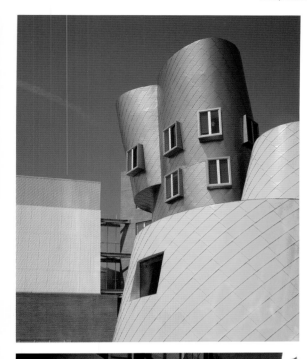

FRANK O. GEHRY & ASSOCIATES / GEHRY PARTNERS

Left: Gehry Partners, MARTa Museum, Herford, Germany, 2005

FRANK O. GEHRY & ASSOCIATES / GEHRY PARTNERS

Gehry Partners, Novartis Campus, Basel, Switzerland, 2009

Gehry Partners, Cleveland Clinic Lou Ruvo Center
for Brain Health, Las Vegas, 2010

FRANK O. GEHRY & ASSOCIATES / GEHRY PARTNERS

Franklin D. Israel Design Associates, Arango-Berry House, Beverly Hills, California, 1989

Franklin D. Israel Design Associates, Goldberg-Bean House, Los Angeles, 1991

FRANKLIN D. ISRAEL

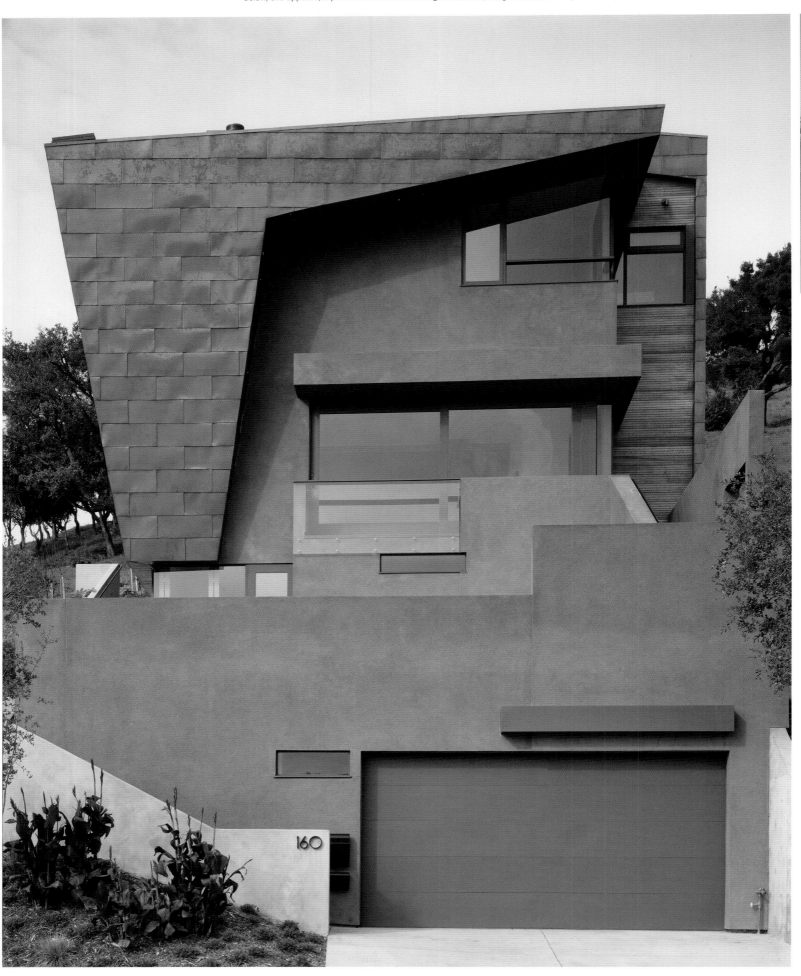

Top right; and bottom: Franklin D. Israel Design Associates, Arango-Berry House, Beverly Hills, California, 1989

FRANKLIN D. ISRAEL

Left, top and bottom: Israel, Callas, Shortridge Design Associates, Dan House, Malibu, California, 1995

Center; and right, top: Franklin D. Israel Design Associates,
Lamy-Newton Pavilion, Los Angeles, 1988

Right, bottom: Israel, Callas, Shortridge Design Associates,
Fine Arts Building, University of California, Riverside, 2001

FRANKLIN D. ISRAEL

Left, top and bottom: Morphosis Architects, Kate Mantilini Restaurant,
Beverly Hills, California, 1986

Morphosis Architects, Landa Residence, Manhattan Beach, California, 1997

MORPHOSIS ARCHITECTS

Morphosis Architects, Blades Residence, Santa Barbara, California, 1997

Morphosis Architects, Diamond Ranch High School, Pomona, California, 1999

Left, top and bottom: Morphosis Architects, Hypo Alpe-Adria Center, Klagenfurt, Austria, 2002

Center; and right: Morphosis Architects, University of Cincinnati Campus Recreation Center,
Cincinnati, Ohio, 2005

Morphosis Architects, Wayne Lyman Morse United States Courthouse, Eugene, Oregon, 2006

Morphosis Architects, Caltrans District 7 Headquarters, Los Angeles, 2004

Below; and opposite, top: Morphosis Architects, Cahill Center for Astronomy and Astrophysics at Caltech, Pasadena, California, 2008

City without Limits: Architectural Innovation and Urban Imaginaries in Los Angeles
Margaret Crawford

Aerial view of downtown Los Angeles and surrounding metropolitan area. Streetscape. Oblique aerial photography, 1956

Photo by Dick Whittington Studio, courtesy of the University of Southern California on behalf of the USC Special Collections

Any attempt at deciphering the connections between Los Angeles and architectural innovation is a challenge. Although many profess that the link exists, few have taken the time to explain it. The numerous observers and interpreters of Los Angeles' urban environment and built form disagree about almost everything. Opinions vary from those who see the city's immensity and fragmentation in dystopic terms, an example of everything a city should not be, to those who celebrate these qualities as a uniquely heterogeneous urbanism that fosters ingenuity and

Aerial view of Los Angeles, 2011

Reyner Banham near Silurian Lake south
of Death Valley in San Bernardino County,
California, 1980

creativity. Every declaration that Los Angeles is unique is met with an equal insistence that it is and should be more like other places. Even during the second decade of the twenty-first century, for every designer attracted to the city as a tabula rasa where anything is possible, there has been another who, seeing only chaos, urges centrality and connections with the past. Some of the best-known beneficiaries of the city's supposed architectural freedom deny that their work has anything to do with its Los Angeles origins. In 1992, Thom Mayne called this "regionalism" and dismissed it as "preposterous."[1] Even the city's most famous architect, Frank O. Gehry, only completed his first major public commission in the city, Walt Disney Concert Hall, in 2003, after several decades of producing major buildings around the globe.

In spite of these difficulties, it is still possible to argue that a recognizable urban imaginary underpins much of the work of the post-Gehry generation. As described by urban scholars, a city's imaginary is a highly selective mental construction made up of collectively shared representations of its urban space, history, and culture. This enabling architectural imaginary is deeply rooted in certain moments in the history of Los Angeles but also responsive to social and economic changes. It is both material—acknowledging the specific conditions that allow buildings to be built here, such as clients, climate, and costs—and imaginary, in its investment in the intangible "atmosphere" of openness and innovation that constitutes this particular architectural culture. Its composite nature allows it to contain both "truth" (empirically verifiable facts), and fiction (invented stories). As a "mental map," it highlights

certain places and qualities while completely disregarding others. Over time, as the city changed, the balance of these elements altered but the overall construct has demonstrated a remarkably enduring power. As much as it has enabled several generations of remarkable architecture, it has also constricted the significance of that architecture in the city at large. Given the magnitude of recent changes in Los Angeles, its continued relevance is an open question.

1973

Reyner Banham established the foundation for this particular understanding of the city in his groundbreaking book, *Los Angeles: The Architecture of Four Ecologies*, first published in 1971. Abandoning the historian's objectivity, Banham explained his fascination with what was then an understudied and underappreciated city, arguing that the very qualities that most observers singled out to attack were actually the city's greatest assets. This began an interpretive argument that continues today. Banham saw the city's vast extent as a thrilling expansiveness rather than sprawl, its divergent architectural forms as visually expressive rather than chaotic, and its multiple centers as representative of diversity rather than fragmentation. What critics depicted as indifference and alienation in the social environment, he interpreted as collective cultural tolerance and a permissive atmosphere. He praised the inhabitants' mobility rather than decrying their auto dependence, naming his fourth ecology "autopia." He singled out the freeway system as the only monument in the city, promoting a new mode of urban perception in which movement itself gave the city unity. This had radical

1. John Chase, "Introduction," *LA 2000+: New Architecture in Los Angeles* (New York: Monacelli Press, 2006), 9.

**Gehry Partners, Walt Disney Concert Hall,
Los Angeles, 2003**

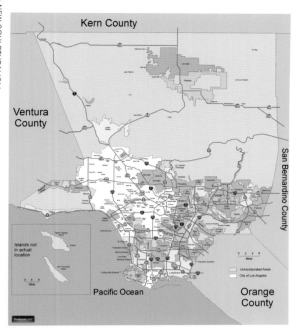

Map of Los Angeles County, 2007
Photo courtesy of Los Angeles Almanac
@ LAAlmanac.com

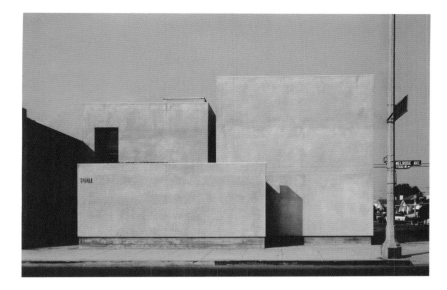

**Frank O. Gehry & Associates, Danziger
Studio/House, West Hollywood, California,
1965**

implications for urbanism. When critics bemoaned the lack of a real downtown, he claimed that, since everywhere was, at least theoretically, close to everywhere else, this eliminated the need for a center.

Banham argued that this unique form of urbanism had generated some of the world's greatest architecture. Although earlier writers like Esther McCoy had celebrated local designers, none had argued for them with Banham's breadth and vehemence. Going far beyond accepted critical norms, he crossed the boundaries between popular culture and high-art architecture, discussing buildings that ranged from Googie coffee shops and dingbats to Spanish Colonial Revival churches and the work of the acclaimed modernists Irving Gill, Rudolph Schindler, Richard Neutra, and Charles Eames. This breadth demonstrated the city's freedom, which encouraged innovation and resulted in not a single Los Angeles style, but in many versions of homegrown modernism. Banham discovered superb modernist houses scattered around the city, mostly along the Pacific shore or hidden in the canyons and winding roads of the foothills. In spite of their excellence, they were largely domestic commissions, noted Banham, while the city's large-scale public or commercial buildings were left to corporate firms.

Most crucially for subsequent architects, Banham identified an architectural imaginary that functioned at two wildly disjunctive scales, the macroscale of the vast conurbation and the microscale of the individual building. For Banham, the city's dispersal and low density offered the practical advantage of open space, "room to maneuver" that provided architects with a sense of potential and agency. Unlike the dense and congested cities of Europe and the East Coast, there was a lot of vacant land available for small buildings of all types. He was astonished by Greater Los Angeles' expanse—seventy square miles not yet filled in—which, viewed from Griffith Park, stretches off almost infinitely south to the harbor. And this was only part of a far larger city whose totality was invisible, extending west and east to the San Fernando and San Gabriel valleys and south to Orange County. Subsequent writers have identified this unprecedented form of urbanism as a new urban aesthetic as compelling in its own way as the vertical skyscraper canyons of Manhattan. As early as the 1920s, a few Angelenos understood that this new mode of modern urbanity had a grandeur that commanded awe, constituting what historian Jeremiah Axelrod called the "horizontal sublime," an infinitely extending metropolis that promised equally endless possibilities.[2] For architects, this produced a paradox: since the city's enormity precluded any notion of architectural intervention on an urban scale, its apparently infinite expanse could function psychologically as a symbolic stand-in for freedom and opportunity.

If the vastness of the region provided an expansive mental context, the scale of the building was where architects actually operated. Although most architectural innovation took place in the limited "ecologies" that Banham identified as "surfurbia" and the "foothills," the vast "plains of id" actually occupied most of the city's territory. While Banham dismissed it as a service area that primarily fed and supplied the foothills and beaches, its endless street corridors also served as an important

2. Jeremiah Axelrod, *Inventing Autopia: Dreams and Visions of the Modern Metropolis in Jazz Age Los Angeles* (Berkeley: University of California Press, 2009), 212–13.

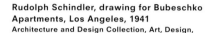

Rudolph Schindler, drawing for Bubeschko
Apartments, Los Angeles, 1941
Architecture and Design Collection, Art, Design, and Architecture Museum, University of California, Santa Barbara

Richard Neutra, Strathmore Apartments,
Los Angeles, 1937
Luckhaus photo, Richard and Dione Neutra Collection, College of Environmental Design, Special Collections, California State Polytechnic University, Pomona

repository of architectural ideas. The city's commercial architecture, often authorless, offered two different models for design: one, the object building, or "duck" identified by Robert Venturi and Denise Scott Brown; the other, the stucco box, the generic "decorated shed." Banham was the first to look seriously at Los Angeles' heritage of historical styles, which came in respectable versions such as the Spanish Colonial Revival auto showrooms or shopping plazas found across the city or implausibly exotic renditions like Grauman's Chinese Theatre. He also traced the evolution of whimsical commercial vernacular styles, as they evolved from the giant hats or hot dogs of the 1920s to the 60s futuristic modernism of the aforementioned Googie coffee shops. These startling sculptural objects stood out against a monotonous cityscape composed of expedient and undistinguished stucco boxes. These could take multiple forms, from the ubiquitous standardized two-story dingbat apartment to an early Gehry building, the Danzinger Studio of 1968, which Banham presciently recognized as an important new synthesis of ordinary streetscape and high-art intentions.

Unlike residents of cities like San Francisco, London, and Paris, who treasured their urban fabric and stock of historic buildings, Angelenos did not value their built environment. In a city with few monuments in the traditional sense, preservation barely existed. This very lack of preciousness encouraged clients and designers to take chances and try something new. In spite of their low status and often-flimsy construction techniques, the extremity of these forms, and the astonishing variety of buildings that served very ordinary purposes set a liberating example.

For architects interested in experimentation, they demonstrated the ability to express strong ideas with limited technical means. In such a heterogeneous visual environment, context could never become a restriction. This knowledge freed adventurous designers to take formal risks unimaginable in more restrictive urban environments.

1993

Twenty years later, Banham's interpretation of the city, echoed over the years by other writers, was so embedded in the general consciousness that many dismissed it as a cliché, historically important but no longer relevant. It described a city whose outlines and destiny had been largely established by the end of the 1920s and was gradually filling in. Change followed existing patterns, and the city became more of what it already was. By 1990 Los Angeles had undergone economic and social changes so dramatic that many feared that the urban identity recognized by Banham was being lost. The regional economy continued to diverge from expected patterns and traditional models. After several rounds of industrial restructuring, it developed along multiple paths, so that no single industry dominated. Although the massive local economy ranked fifteenth in the world, its growth was unevenly distributed. The entertainment and ports industries thrived while factory closings decimated others. The appearance of large numbers of low-wage immigrant workers strained existing labor markets, particularly among African American men. The 1990 census listed more than 40 percent of adults in South Central Los Angeles as "not in the labor market."[3] Combined with the real estate market's volatile boom and bust cycles, this regularly

3. Susan Anderson, "A City Called Heaven: Black Enchantment and Despair in Los Angeles," in *The City: Los Angeles and Urban Theory at the End of the Twentieth Century* (Berkeley: University of California Press, 1996), 340.

**Franklin D. Israel Design Associates, Drager
House, Berkeley, California, 1994**

produced serious regional recessions. The impact of these fluctuations was felt most by those at the bottom, widening the gap between rich and poor.

The expanding economy and the region's traditional attractions brought immigrants from all over the world, with the majority from Mexico, Central America, and Asia. They transformed the city's racial and ethnic makeup, which went from 81 percent white in 1960 to 43 percent in 2000,[4] becoming one of the first majority minority cities. In 1990, 40 percent of the population was born outside of the Unites States.[5] Although Latinos predominated, there were significant Chinese, Korean, Filipino, Armenian, Russian, Iranian, and Israeli communities, making the region the most diverse in the country. Rapid population growth pushed settlement outward to the city's natural boundaries. Inside them, residents were unevenly distributed according to class and ethnicity but, at the same time, continually in flux. Many Mexican immigrants settled in the traditional East Los Angeles barrio while those from Oaxaca preferred Santa Monica and the Westside. New arrivals from Central America stayed in the MacArthur Park area to save money, then began to buy houses in Watts, previously all African American. After realtors marketed Monterey Park as the "Chinese Beverly Hills," the adjacent San Gabriel Valley towns, once completely white, then primarily Latino, became predominantly Asian.

The tension produced by this unprecedented degree of ethnic diversity and economic disparity convinced many Angelenos that the city would

not survive. Urban critic Mike Davis's *City of Quartz: Excavating the Future in Los Angeles*, published in 1990, and David Rieff's 1991 *Los Angeles: Capital of the Third World* both depicted the city in apocalyptic terms, seeing the visible and invisible boundaries of class, race, ethnicity, and religion as symptoms of a collapsing public realm and a multiethnic city on the verge of implosion. The urban disturbances of 1991 and 1992 appeared to confirm their fears. The verdicts in the Latasha Harlins and Rodney King trials unleashed an outpouring of anger, reflecting Los Angeles' intricate social landscape, in which cultures reacted and interacted in complex and unpredictable ways. African Americans called the uprising the "justice riots," attacking the racism of the criminal justice system. Others responded to economic issues such as poverty and unemployment, exacerbated by recession. The disturbances dramatized the city's tangled racial dynamics. Fifty-one percent of those arrested were Hispanic while only 34 percent were African American. Immigrants were pitted against one another and Korean stores were targets for much of the burning and looting that ensued during the riots.[6]

It is clear that the prevailing architectural imaginary could not accommodate these events and issues. Critic Charles Jencks argued that avant-garde practitioners such as Gehry, Eric Owen Moss, Morphosis Architects, and Franklin D. Israel literally mirrored the city's fractures in the colliding and splintering fragments of their buildings, but this interpretation mistakes compositional strategies for symbolism.[7] The torqued steel assemblages typical of Morphosis' work during this era, often likened to the dystopian film *Blade Runner*, might be seen as an emblem

4. James P. Allen and Eugene Turner, *The Ethnic Quilt: Population Diversity in Southern California* (Los Angeles: The Center for Geographical Studies, 1997), 45–49.

5. Ibid., 44.
6. "Understanding the Riots," *Los Angeles Times*, May 11 and 13, 1992.

7. Charles Jencks, *Heteropolis: Los Angeles, the Riots and the Strange Beauty of Hetero-Architecture* (London: St. Martin's Press, 1993), 24–30.

**Frank O. Gehry & Associates, Chiat/Day
Building, Los Angeles, 1991**

of urban angst if they had not been created for the benign spaces of restaurants and clinics and explicitly intended to "communicate compassion and confidence."[8] But even if architects registered the urban zeitgeist, their responses were indirect, distanced, and hermetic. Even Davis's attacks on Gehry and other architects for designing a fortified city excluding the poor and homeless had little resonance.[9] Since the riots primarily took place in the "plains of id," they barely impacted the sites of architectural culture.

At the same time, as this exhibition demonstrates, these years were extraordinarily rich and productive for formal exploration in architecture. Gehry, in a series of small but daring local buildings, especially his own 1978 house, opened up an arena for experimentation that younger architects enthusiastically occupied. But they continued to practice in a context that mirrored the economic, social, and spatial patterns of architectural innovation in Los Angeles, in the early twentieth century. Architects worked individually in small firms, limiting their technical capabilities. Most of their buildings were still single-family houses, along with boutiques, galleries, and restaurants. Many of the urban changes produced benefits both real and imagined. Los Angeles' new image as a world-class if troubled city heightened a sense of possibility, raising the architectural stakes considerably. Immigration expanded a client base of open-minded but not necessarily rich people, bringing not only the poor and striving but also large numbers of wealthy individuals, many involved in creative industries. Teaching positions at Southern California Institute of Architecture, University of California Los Angeles, and University of

Southern California provided financial security, allowing designers to survive between jobs. In spite of these advances, just like their modernist predecessors, avant-garde designers remained marginal to the city at large. As always, when major commissions came along, the city's conservative establishment usually awarded them to corporate offices or, for important public buildings, outside designers.

2013

By 2010 there were indications that this historic model of innovative practice might no longer be tenable. If a culture of architectural innovation was going to continue, a new urban imaginary would be necessary. Many of the enabling conditions that Banham identified forty years earlier had vanished, prompting competing visions for the city's future. Greater Los Angeles had expanded far beyond the seventy square miles that had astonished Banham to nearly 5,000 square miles. If this even vaster extent might still be sublime, it was no longer infinite. Once the city reached its spatial limits, development doubled back and started filling in the remaining city. Even more startling, in 2010 the U.S. census announced that Los Angeles was the densest metropolitan area in the country. The significance of this fact was ambiguous, since it only measured population density. Los Angeles was still decentralized and its spatial density was unevenly distributed. Although some districts were visibly overcrowded, much of the city, as critic Christopher Hawthorne noted, contained large numbers of vacant lots. The center of downtown, cleared for urban renewal in the 1960s, was still waiting for redevelopment.[10]

8. From the "Morphopedia" index of projects on Morphosis Architects' website, available at: www.morphopedia.com/projects/cedars-sinai-comprehensive-cancer-center. Accessed September 1, 2012.

9. Mike Davis, *City of Quartz: Excavating the Future in Los Angeles* (New York: Verso, 1990), 78.

10. Christopher Hawthorne, "Contemporary Voice: Thickets of Diversity, Swaths of Emptyness," in *A Companion to Los Angeles*, eds. William Deverell and Greg Hise (London: Blackwell-Wiley, 2010), 481.

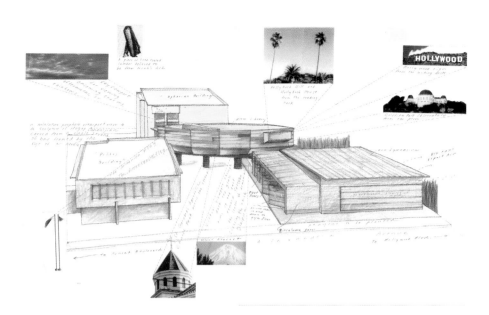

Studio Works Architects, diagram for Pilibos School Library and Gymnasium, Los Angeles, 2006

Still, the threat and promise of density renewed decades-old demands that Los Angeles should be more like other cities. The perception of a newly dense city provided ammunition for visions of a Manhattan-like downtown, dense with skyscrapers and high-rise condos. In 2008, supported by the downtown corporate elite, large-scale developers, the city's Community Redevelopment Agency, urban planners, and citizens, billionaire Eli Broad hired Gehry to design its core, Grand Avenue. The irony of the architect who best embodied the city's freedom now designing an entire downtown further weakened an urban imaginary that celebrated the lack of a conventional urban center.[11]

Similarly, the automobility that defined the city for Banham was also in question. In spite of its popular image, by 2010 Greater Los Angeles had fewer freeways per capita than any major city.[12] Massive population growth produced traffic problems so serious that Los Angeles ranked first in the nation for congestion delays. Starting in the late 1980s, the Metropolitan Transit Authority had begun an ambitious transit program, combining new commuter rail, subway, and light-rail lines into a system that covered eighty-seven miles. Buses still served a far larger number of riders, with service that improved significantly over the last decade. Bottom-up transit solutions also flourished, with bike riders and pedestrians proliferating, even among groups with access to automobiles. Events like CicLAvia and organizations like LA Walks popularize nonautomotive uses of the city's streets.

In the 1970s, Banham saw the city shaping architecture, not the other way around. However, beginning around 2000, a number of factors came together to offer architects larger public roles. As Los Angeles' politics became more diverse, a new power structure emerged. Antonio Villaraigosa became the city's first Latino mayor in 130 years, and large swaths of Korean, Chinese, and Latino homeowners began to elect officials who reflected their values. Gehry's national recognition and the enormous popular success of Walt Disney Concert Hall (2003) produced a ripple effect that benefited architectural innovation in general. This encouraged institutional clients to extend important commissions to local architects that would have been unthinkable a few decades earlier, such as Thom Mayne's selection for the Caltrans headquarters. Both buildings, despite their urban settings, extend the tradition of object buildings to a monumental scale rather than propose new ways of relating to their surroundings.

Other institutions such as colleges, universities, and municipal governments followed their lead, with commissions that not only offered innovative architects a presence in the public realm but demanded engagement with new immigrant populations as users, if not clients. In 1998 population growth pushed the Los Angeles Unified School District to begin a major school construction program, hiring a surprising number of adventurous architects, including Studio Works Architects, Morphosis Architects, and Hodgetts + Fung. Other schools, libraries, and small public buildings proliferated, making new architecture both visible and usable in all parts of the city and for the first time, an accepted part of the public realm. In addition, increased density and the rising cost of land prompted private and nonprofit developers to produce more

11. Cara Mia DiMassa, "Grand Avenue Project," *Los Angeles Times*, April 24, 2006.

12. Paul Sorensen, "Moving Los Angeles," *Access* 35 (Fall 2009): 26–30.

multifamily housing for all sectors of the population, ranging from luxury condos to affordable housing or even homeless shelters. For the same reasons, commercial projects have grown in size and scale, allowing designers to take on more complex projects and sites. Architectural interest in the city beyond the building is also growing, as books speculating on the city's urban future, by prominent practitioners such as Mayne and Michael Maltzan, demonstrate.[13]

What is still lacking, however, is an interpretation of the city's current reality that can transform these changed conditions into an operative imaginary. Design freedom is now found in many places, most notably inside a computer. The isolation that Gehry found liberating is no longer possible. These new circumstances will make it difficult to find a version of freedom situated in the conditions that define Los Angeles today. The city's inexhaustible multiplicity and diversity suggest other dimensions to freedom than fulfilling a personal vision. Even if actual mobility is stalled, unlimited mental movement across the boundaries of the city's microgeographies is still possible. This challenges architects to finally abandon their enclaves for once and for all, in order to discover and reimagine how the city could support a new kind of innovation.

13. See Richard Koshalek, Thom Mayne, and Dana Hutt, L.A. Now: Volume One (Los Angeles: University of California Press, 2002); and Michael Maltzan, No More Play: Conversations on Urban Space in Los Angeles and Beyond (Ostfildern, Germany: Hatje Cantz, 2011).

Top: RoTo Architects, CDLT 1, 2, Los Angeles, 1992   Bottom: RoTo Architects, New Jersey House, Bernardsville, New Jersey, 1996   **ROTO ARCHITECTS**

Top and bottom: RoTo Architects, Carlson-Reges House, Los Angeles, 1996

Top: RoTo Architects, aerial view of Carlson-Reges House, Los Angeles, 1996

Bottom: RoTo Architects, Warehouse C, Nagasaki, Japan, 1997

Below; and opposite, bottom: RoTo Architects, Architecture and Art Building, Prairie View A & M University, Prairie View, Texas, 2005

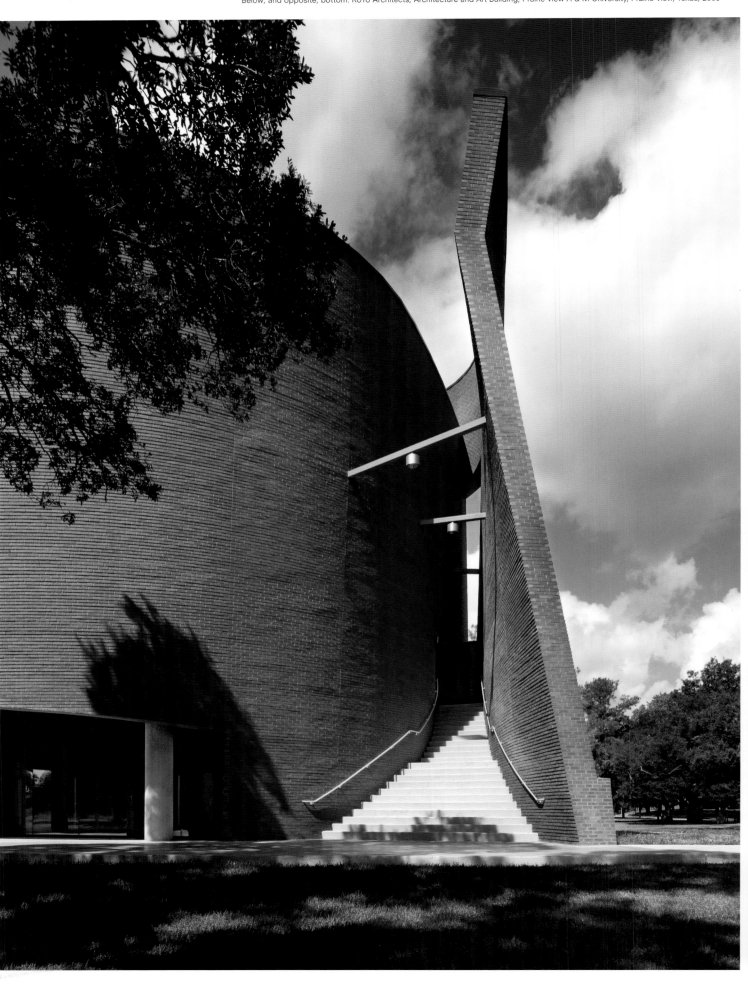

Top: RoTo Architects, in collaboration with JAG Architects, Madame Tussauds Hollywood, Los Angeles, 2009

Left, top: Saee Studio, Angeli Trattoria, Los Angeles, 1986

Left, bottom: Saee Studio, 434 Apartments, Los Angeles, 1989

Center: Saee Studio, Publicis Drugstore, Paris, 2004

Right, top and bottom: Saee Studio, Linnie House, Los Angeles, 2004

Eric Owen Moss Architects, Lawson-Westen House, Los Angeles, 1993

ERIC OWEN MOSS ARCHITECTS

Left, bottom: Eric Owen Moss Architects, The Box, Culver City, California, 1994

Left, top; and below: Eric Owen Moss Architects, Stealth, Culver City, California, 2001

ERIC OWEN MOSS ARCHITECTS

Below: Eric Owen Moss Architects, rendering of Jefferson Tower, Los Angeles, 2014 (projected completion)

Bottom: Eric Owen Moss Architects, photomontage of Pterodactyl, Culver City, California, 2013

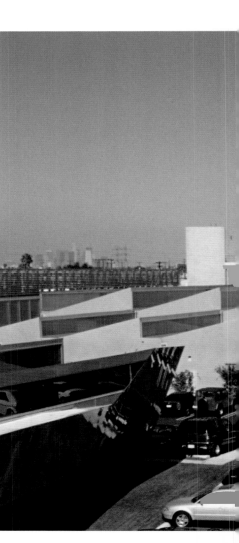

VOID, Bobco Metals Co., Los Angeles, 2004

Where There's a Will, There's a Way: Conversations with Clients in Southern California
Johanna Vandemoortele

Frank O. Gehry & Associates,
Gehry Residence, Santa Monica,
California, 1977 (before reconstruction)

**Morphosis Architects,
Venice III,
Los Angeles, 1986**

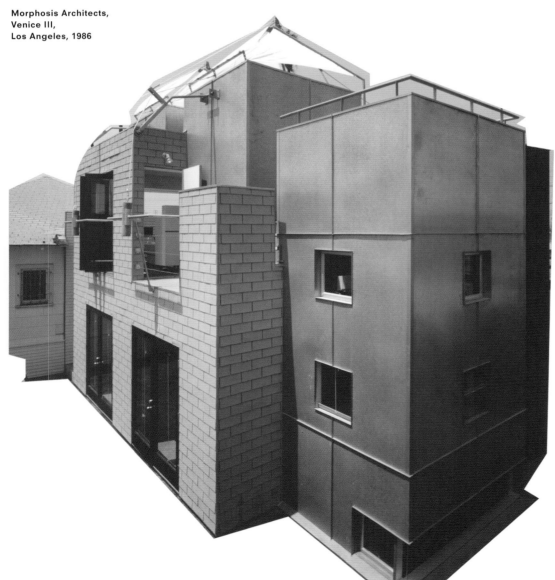

For more than a century, Southern California has cultivated and sustained a reputation as a seedbed for experimentation and invention in residential architecture. The presence of many noteworthy homes in Los Angeles solidifies the notion that the residential sphere is a strong contender within the ring of architectural form-making in the city. Drawing from interviews with the clients who commissioned some of these landmark homes in the past three decades, this essay examines why so many residential projects in Los Angeles seem to benefit from a distinct freedom of expression and form as compared with other cities in the United States, with a focus on the clients themselves and their key relationships with the architects who have designed their homes.

The house as a testing ground for ideas of form, materiality, and technology has been a recurring concept in architecture for many years. As Esther McCoy wrote in her introduction to *Case Study Houses: 1945–1962*, "contemporary design [has] never been in quarantine in California—the West Coast [is] one of the great proving grounds."[1] This combination of Los Angeles' fertile ground

1. Esther McCoy, *Case Study Houses: 1945–1962*, rev. ed. (Santa Monica, Calif.: Hennessey + Ingalls, 1977), 9.

Frank O. Gehry & Associates,
Gehry Residence, Santa Monica,
California, 1978/94

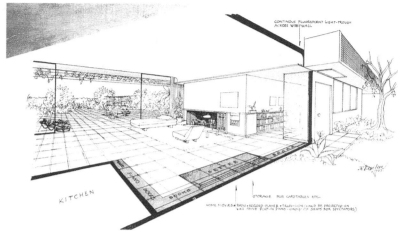

Plan from J. R. Davidson, "Case Study
House #1," article in *Arts & Architecture*
magazine, March 1945

for experimentation and the house as test subject for new ideas and design concepts has led to a variety of spectacular residences across Southern California over the past century. These houses have also become key projects in the success stories of many architects; in several cases, the architects have served as their own clients in order to turn their dreams into reality. Frank O. Gehry's home, a pink 1920s bungalow in Santa Monica that he drastically remodeled in the late 70s, is a well-known example of the architect-as-client model.

In her 1989 Museum of Contemporary Art, Los Angeles, exhibition "Blueprints for Modern Living: History and Legacy of the Case Study Houses" and her subsequent publications on the Case Study House (CSH) program, Elizabeth A. T. Smith makes sure to place the CSH project within the previously recognized traditions of residential architecture across the United States as well as the already established experimental context of Los Angeles itself. Smith and McCoy trace the CSH program back through the residential architecture of Irving Gill, Rudolph Schindler, Frank Lloyd Wright, Richard Neutra, Julius Ralph Davidson, and many others, arguing that the two-decade-long experimental house series, which *Arts & Architecture* magazine launched in 1945, was not "an isolated phenomenon but…an episode in a wider architectural history."[2]

In addition to the CSH program, there were several other examples of concerted public and cultural efforts to examine new conceptions of the American family home. These included the fifteen prototypes built for the

Town of Tomorrow at the 1939 New York World's Fair; Wright's Usonian House; a temporary pavilion of a "completely furnished two-bedroom house"[3] presented in 1953 by the Solomon R. Guggenheim Foundation, New York; as well as exhibition houses built by architects Marcel Breuer and Gregory Ain at the Museum of Modern Art, New York (MoMA), in 1949 and 1950, respectively. In their press release publicizing Ain's design, MoMA announced that the house "was built…to demonstrate that good modern architectural design is possible in the speculatively built house, which is the kind lived in by most American families."[4] These examples, however, while showcasing ideas for the contemporary home, present a product missing one major component: a real user, the client. Even John Entenza, who championed the CSH program as editor of *Arts & Architecture*, wrote in its inaugural announcement that "Architects will be responsible to no one but the magazine, which having put on a long white beard, will pose as 'client.' It is to be clearly understood that every consideration will be given to new materials and new techniques in house construction."[5] This attitude certainly allowed for an unprecedented development of new ideas and invention in residential construction, but the idealized notion of bringing these houses beyond the protected client structure and to the masses never took root. As Dolores Hayden wrote, "For all the rhetoric they produced on 'standardization' and 'the low-cost house,' [the] creations were individualistic and expensive."[6]

This underlines the argument that there needs to be a participating and willing client for the success of innovative architecture to take shape. Architectural critic and journalist Mariana Griswold Van Rensselaer's

2. Elizabeth A. T. Smith, "Icons of Mid-Century Modernism: The Case Study Houses," in *Case Study Houses: The Complete CHS Program 1945–1966*, ed. Smith and Peter Goessel (Cologne: Taschen, 2002), 8.
3. Press release, "Sixty Years of Living Architecture Exhibition," The Solomon R. Guggenheim Foundation, New York, October 20, 1953, 1.

4. Press release, "Exhibition House to Open In Museum Garden on May 19," The Museum of Modern Art, New York, May 1, 1950, 1.
5. John Entenza, "Announcement: The Case Study House Program," *Arts & Architecture* 62, no. 1 (January 1945): 38.

6. Dolores Hayden,"Model Houses for the Millions: Architects' Dreams, Builders' Boasts, Residents' Dilemmas," in *Blueprints for Modern Living: History and Legacy of the Case Study Houses*, ed. Elizabeth A. T. Smith, exh. cat. (Los Angeles: Museum of Contemporary Art, 1989), 209.

**Morphosis Architects, Venice III,
Los Angeles, 1986**

**Daly Genik Architects, Palms House,
Los Angeles, 2011**

observation in her 1890 essay "Client and Architect" is as relevant today as it was more than 120 years ago:

> [The inevitable difference between the architect and artist] is the natural result of the fact that architecture is not an art pure and simple. It has a practical side. Its products are not mere objects of beauty. They are useful objects made beautiful, and they cannot be spun out of the artist's brain, but must cost a great deal of money. When useful, costly things which take up a deal of space are in question, demand must precede supply.[7]

So where is this demand coming from? Who is building these "useful objects made beautiful," and why in Southern California and Los Angeles in particular?[8]

This essay presents responses from interviews with more than fifteen clients of different architects in Los Angeles. They begin to shed light on some of the reasons why such avant-garde residential architecture is more prevalent in Southern California than in any other part of the country. The interviews not only yield interesting anecdotes and unique characteristics about particular homes and architects, but they also reveal some general trends about the story of clients in Southern California over the past thirty years.

California: Trials and Dreams

"We were all very young and foolish."
—Ann Bergren, client of Morphosis, Venice III, 1982–86

In 1949 journalist Carey McWilliams wrote, "The fact is that Californians have become so used to the idea of experimentation…they are psychologically prepared to try anything. Experience has taught them that almost 'anything' might work in California; you never know."[9] This idea, that California represents a place where dreams can be born if you "just try it" still drives many who make their way to Los Angeles today. Several of the architects and clients discussed here are originally from elsewhere, a common characteristic of Angelenos, as the city is one of the largest and most diverse in the country.

Ann Bergren is a professor in the Department of Classics at the University of California, Los Angeles (UCLA). She lives in a renovated 1920s Venice Beach home with a 1986 addition by Morphosis Architects, which then comprised the team of Thom Mayne and Michael Rotondi. Bergren had recently moved to Los Angeles before starting the addition, and she explains, "In the 1960s there was the notion of the megalopolis, and it was Boston, New York, Philadelphia, and Washington. Before I came to California to work for UCLA, I was from megalopolis. I have many layers of life there and I arrived here to teach [in] 1980." A short while later, needing more space and having been profoundly drawn to two of their other residential projects, the Sedlack Residence (1981) and 2-4-6-8 House (1978), Bergren commissioned Mayne and Rotondi to build an addition

7. Marianna Griswold Van Rensselaer, "Client and Architect," *The North American Review* 151, no. 406 (September 1890): 319.

8. I use "Southern California" and "Los Angeles" interchangeably, as is common in the literature on the architecture of the region.

9. Carey McWilliams, *California: The Great Exception* (Westport, Conn.: Greenwood Press, 1949), 221–22.

Morphosis Architects, view of guest
bathroom from libary, Venice III,
Los Angeles, 1986

Daly Genik Architects, Palms House,
Los Angeles, 2011

to her existing home. As she states, "The ideal situation is that you would see something by an architect and you would so love it or identify with it that you would be able to say 'Do exactly what you want.'" Bergren further touches on this in a piece she wrote for *House & Garden* magazine in 1986:

> After seeing two small black-and-white pictures in a magazine of the Sedlack and 2-4-6-8 houses (two other additions in Venice with which my place makes a sort of triptych and so is called Venice III), all I wanted was for Michael and Thom to build what they wanted to, and they did. But without realizing it, I must have seen in those pictures a reflection of my own intellectual and aesthetic disposition, for just by effacing myself as a designer in the project, I have gotten the sort of classic I would have designed.[10]

In recalling the project, she explains that "this was an experimental piece; they experimented with things and I understand that." There is an unmistakable optimism in her memories of the process, and she admits that "they were learning, we were all very young and foolish, and we were all about the same age." This youthful, fearless, and almost playful energy is essentially Californian. While open and unassuming, Bergren's addition is not a quiet or shy space, and it exhibits multiple moments in which the architects diverted from the conventional use of materials or programmatic juxtapositions. Roof shingles and exterior siding are used in the master bedroom, and at certain points in the house, there appear somewhat unsettling yet crucial relationships, such as a guest bathroom looking directly onto the living room library, a moment Bergren herself

studied for her portfolio when later applying to architecture schools. As Bergren wrote about her home in *House & Garden*, "Form here becomes dynamically ambiguous, obscuring the demarcation between inner and outer structures. It is a pleasure to reread the confident risk of this spatial arrangement every time I walk through it."[11]

The idea of experimentation is still very much alive, albeit often with more advanced and expensive materials than were available thirty years ago. When television and movie writer Sam Laybourne and news producer Herran Bekele first arrived in Los Angeles from New York in the early 2000s, Venice gave them "a sense of Brooklyn by the Sea" that attracted them. The couple had the opportunity to co-own a property with Laybourne's parents and in 2005 found a plot in Venice containing two structures with a garden in-between. Needing more room and wanting to create a home for themselves with an additional guesthouse for visiting family, they chose Daly Genik Architects to update the property. Principal Kevin Daly kept the basic plot footprint. As Laybourne explains, "We really wanted to keep the idea of the two structures, and Kevin's idea, the one that really got us to select him and excited about using him, was the concept of two lanterns hovering in the beautiful courtyard. The idea of metal-wrapped skins got us very excited and started the process." From this initial idea, which is very much an object-based conception, Daly Genik Architects experimented with material and form to shape a sculptural inner courtyard framed by the expressive metal mesh forms of two engaging and lighthearted structures. Completed in 2011, Palms House now includes the main family house

10. Ann Bergren, "Interplay of Opposites: Thom Mayne and Michael Rotondi's Ingenious Addition to an Alley House in Venice, California," *House & Garden* (January 1986): 128.

11. Bergren, 132.

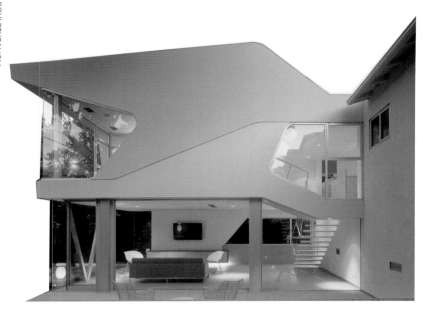

**Neil M. Denari Architects, Alan-Voo House,
Los Angeles, 2007**

**Neil M. Denari Architects, Alan-Voo House,
Los Angeles, 2007**

for Laybourne, Bekele, and their young children, and a guesthouse, sometimes used as an office. Laybourne and Bekele are keenly aware that throughout the neighborhood,

> [P]eople are trying some really neat things, it's a place where amazing architects have incubated projects on small land parcels, which is an interesting public works concept because it leaves little gems throughout the city, and it's fun to be a part of that bigger legacy. There is something rogue about Venice, there's no real sense of aesthetic rules, and you get some really crazy choices that don't work and you get a lot that do, and that's fun, we like being in a place people are allowed to fail a little bit.

In 2004, Eric Alan, a movie marketer, and his wife, Rhonda Voo, an artist and illustrator, commissioned architect Neil M. Denari to design an addition to their Los Angles home of more than a decade. A few years prior, the Alan-Voo family had participated in a UCLA anthropological study on middle-class households in Southern California. This research followed the lives, homes, and routines of thirty-two families in Los Angeles.[12] It was an eye-opening experience for the family, who quickly realized they wanted to release themselves from the clutter they had become so accustomed to in the past. With three daughters, the couple decided they needed a solution to their less-than-1,200-square-foot, one-bathroom house, and subsequently began their search for an architect to remedy the problem. After visiting Denari's L.A. Eyeworks (2002) in Los Angeles, the couple experienced a very personal reaction toward the space.

As Alan explains,

> I'll never forget the first time I approached L.A. Eyeworks, and all the little cues of 'Oh my god…it can't be this good…wait a minute.' We looked at all the details and the exterior and thought, 'This was done by a genius. Whoever did this is a genius.' Perhaps it was our attraction to that and the feeling we got in the space, kind of like you were drunk, it was euphoric. I think the experience of living in clutter, of living in the chaos of raising three kids, is why we found that feeling attractive. It felt serene, it felt clean, it felt ethereal, and it felt like we were up in the clouds.

This response prompted Alan and Voo to contact Denari and begin the process of reimagining their home. As a marketer, Alan shared a personal brand language for their family as a jumping-off point to start communicating with Denari:

> Family Brand Attributes: Artsy but not artsy-fartsy; cultured but not elitist; spontaneous but not disorderly; creative but not obsessively so; informal but not messy; into macs + iPods but not techie; enjoys the finer things of life but not extravagantly.

> Strategy: Stay connected as a family; grow as individuals; live in "the now"; encourage the enjoyment of momentary pleasures; remain flexible; anticipate family's future needs; connect to the natural environment.

12. This research was recently published by the Cotsen Institute of Archaeology at UCLA, entitled *Life at Home in the Twenty-First Century: 32 Families Open Their Doors* (Jeanne Arnold, Anthony P. Graesch, Enzo Ragazzini, and Elinor Ochs).

**Eric Owen Moss Architects, Lawson-Westen
House, Los Angeles, 1993**

Tactics: Create privacy realms for individuals; create public realms
to encourage "elbow-rubbing" opportunities; provide multi-use
"flex space" for varied family activities; create a sanctuary to
counter-balance the daily stress of the outside world; reduce clutter;
connect to backyard by creating an outdoor living room; Provide
ample + convenient storage.

California historian Kevin Starr has written that throughout the history of
the state, "clients [have] subsumed their personal histories and dreams
into architecture."[13] Alan and Voo would categorize this mining of
dreams as a quintessential part of what makes their home so
"Los Angeles." As Alan says, "I know how hard it is to get a dream
into reality, to turn a dream into something physical. I tell you what, that
probably makes [our house] the most LA of all, that you just have to
make a commitment that you're going to turn a dream, a vision, a plan,
into an actually physical reality." To which Voo adds, "and then you get
to live in it, it's amazing." Today, the Alan-Voo House (2007) is testament
to their release of clutter, with minimal furniture, many built-in fixtures,
and a remarkable lack of "stuff." The family has let go of so much that a
slight echo joins most conversations, but to them, this is a small price to
pay for the serenity the house offers. This notion of having a dream, an
idea of progress and advancement, a different and changing future—is a
view that many of the other clients share.

The Genius and the Users

"We wanted to live inside of a sculpture."
—Tracy Westen, client of Eric Owen Moss Architects, Lawson-Westen
House, 1993

Having a progressive client, however, is only one part of the equation
that allows for such expressive, avant-garde residential architecture
to exist in Southern California. The architect, the artist molding these
"useful objects," must also work in an environment that allows for
individual authenticity to be exhibited in their signature homes. Tracy
Westen, a public policy lawyer who selected Eric Owen Moss to build
his home in Los Angeles in the early 1990s, felt that Los Angeles then
held sufficient isolation as a city for individual creativity to be nurtured.
As a "city of separate communities networked together by freeways,"
he explains, Los Angeles allowed for each architect's personal imagination to be cultivated instead of "becoming co-opted by everyone else's
mainstream views." For their own home, Westen and his wife, Linda
Lawson, first conducted a lengthy research process into many contemporary California architects, forming their own opinions on their work
as well as reaching out to people such as the late *Los Angeles Times*
architecture critic John Dreyfuss. After meeting with eleven architects,
the last of whom was Franklin D. Israel, and receiving warnings from
Dreyfuss that Moss might be "too radical" for them, Westen convinced
his wife that they should meet with Moss. Lawson herself had had
initial reservations about his work, having only seen photographs of his
projects throughout their research. When recalling their first meeting on

13. Kevin Starr, *Coast of Dreams: California on the Edge, 1990–
2003* (New York: Knopf, 2004), 56.

Eric Owen Moss Architects, Lawson-Westen
House, Los Angeles, 1993

Patrick Tighe Architecture, Gelner Residence,
Mar Vista, California, 2008

a Saturday in Culver City, Westen says:

> Within a few minutes, we were very engaged…he was different
> than anyone we had met…Suddenly, it seemed to me, we were in
> another realm of creativity. Everyone resonates with different things,
> but suddenly we were seeing things we had not seen before. At that
> point, I sketched out some ideas and Eric would take them and say
> "Well you could do this" and start drawing on my drawing upside
> down. For a few minutes we had an interactive process, which we
> hadn't had with anyone else. He would just take the idea and begin
> changing it.

Following the meeting, and after experiencing some of Moss's projects
in person, Lawson had also been convinced and it was she who ultimately asked Moss to design their home. The interactive process of that
first encounter foreshadowed the design phase of the house. As Westen

says, "We'd come in saying maybe the kitchen ought to look like this,
and Eric would say 'OK, but you could also do this, and do that.' He was
a genius, he was a genius, but he interacted with you and you just saw
the Mozart emerging. In other words, he would take something amateur
and he would transform it into something spectacular."

The notion of the architect as a genius, or sole artist, was not uncommon
when speaking to the clients, who often had very personal and emotional
experiences accompanying their decisions to choose their architects. Alan
and Voo call Denari "a genius, a real poet." Patrick Tighe, who has built
single-family houses such as the Tigertail and Gelner residences (both
2008) as well as multiple-family affordable housing in West Hollywood, has
had both types of clients refer to him as a "genius" or "visionary." Kendra
Gelner, whose Tighe-designed house is in Mar Vista, admits that her family
"bought this house purely for the house. It could have been anywhere, in
any neighborhood. All the things we had been so focused on before just
didn't seem to matter. We wanted THIS house…. He is a genius." Ryan
Burns, who with his wife, Aline Nakashima, chose XTEN Architecture to
completely remodel a 1960s home in Hollywood in 2010, noted that "as
for the design, we had a general concept in mind, a house open to the
elements (the existing home [had] tiny windows throughout, and not one of
them faced the iconic 'Hollywood' sign, which was completely mind-bog-
gling). XTEN took that concept and ran with it." Bergren attributes her
only moment of authorship in Venice III to seeing Morphosis's Sedlack
Residence and 2-4-6-8 House and deciding from those projects that
Morphosis was the right fit for her. The rest, she says, was "completely

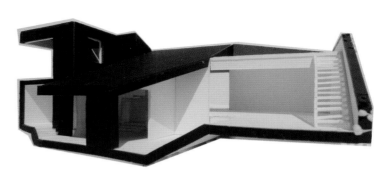

**Daly Genik Architects, Winnett,
Santa Monica, California, 2007**

**XTEN Architecture, process model for
Nakahouse, Los Angeles 2010**

Thom and Michael." Allen Yamashita, who, along with his partner, commissioned Daly Genik Architects to design their home in Santa Monica, wrote:

> As a filmmaker, I am familiar with the creative/design process, so though neither my partner nor I knew anything about architecture per se, we understood that everything starts with a clear idea, followed by imagining that idea through a prescribed set of materials, and then realizing it through a process incorporating craftsmanship, discipline, and a certain amount of flexibility to allow for unanticipated discoveries and revelations. Simply put, we understood that if we wanted to have a chance at realizing a good house, the whole thing starts with a talented architect.

Such responses, among many others, highlight the clients' awareness that in choosing these architects, they are, in some way, handing over aesthetic ownership of their homes.

This does not mean, however, that these clients played no role in the design process toward the final product of architecture that they themselves would live in. In fact, in the words of Cesar Pelli, "Good clients are needed more than ever, but today that means people who care about the building and the art; are involved through the whole design process; are explicit in their needs and goals, likes and dislikes; and make clear and timely decisions."[14] This was a common thread throughout the client interviews, although the spectrum of demands from clients ranged between the poles of feeling and function. Westen,

in working with Moss, describes the design process in different parts:

> Eric asked us to write him a letter, so we did, and we realized that in retrospect we talked more about feelings than about spaces. We never said, for instance, we want three bedrooms, a dining room, a living room—we never said what we wanted, which is actually kind of weird, it just didn't occur to us. Instead we said we wanted a house with an inside-outside feel…because we were in Southern California, we wanted to be connected to the outside. We wanted a house that had fewer large spaces rather than a lot of small spaces; we liked space and we wanted a sense of volume. I think I said that I liked eccentric sources of light, just interesting places for light to come through. We said we wanted places to put our art. We wanted a spiritual feeling to the house, a sense of meditation and calm…a sense of tranquility and peace. We said we liked warmth and color, we didn't want a sterile glass and steel house. We said the kitchen had to be the center of the house…We also said we wanted to live inside a sculpture.

While these requests seem to focus more on the emotional than on the functional, as they began delving deeper into the design, Lawson and Westen found themselves "deferring to Eric's aesthetic judgments almost exclusively, [but were] insistent on matters of function and practicality." Alan and Voo also recall that while they were very open to Denari's work, they "would absolutely give feedback if there was a functional issue" and when the *New York Times* highlighted Daly Genik's Palms House, Herran

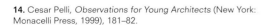
14. Cesar Pelli, *Observations for Young Architects* (New York: Monacelli Press, 1999), 181–82.

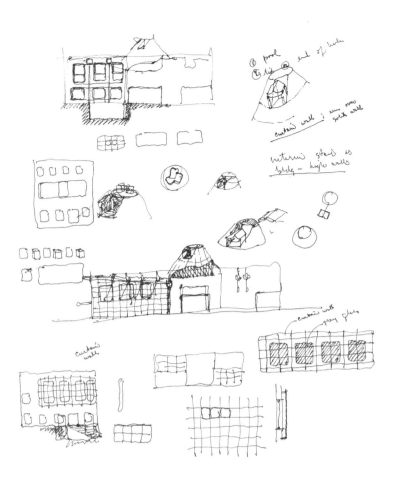

**Eric Owen Moss Architects,
sketch for Lawson-Westen House,
Los Angeles, 1993**

**Patrick Tighe Architecture,
Sierra Bonita Mixed Use Affordable
Housing, West Hollywood, California, 2010**

admits to a slight learning curve regarding aesthetics and function. Speaking about the Sierra Bonita project, Conerly says:

> Everyone was so taken by the design, it was on the front of magazines, we were getting awards, it was all wonderful, but for the residents, the user, we felt we could make some improvements, which John Mutlow and Patrick Tighe have made on the new building, the La Brea Courtyard. It still has a lovely aesthetic, but as the developer, where we came in was to guide them a little more in terms of what the residents needed to feel comfortable in the building. Yes, to live in a beautiful building is really a wonderful thing for everybody, it gives them a certain pride of ownership and excitement to be where they are, but you know, the kitchen also has to function.

Bekele described the process as one in which "the architects got to keep their point of view [and] we got the things we needed."[15] Eric Grunbaum, who commissioned Barbara Bestor to design his home in Venice, writes that as "an Executive Creative Director in advertising…although I had no personal expertise in architecture, it's safe to assume that I was a very involved client. That said, the concept and design was all Barbara's." He continues to say that the house, "feels good to be in…whether it is the light, the craftsmanship, the unfussy-but-warm materials, or the idiosyncratic design, I love coming home to this place."

Even in larger projects such as West Hollywood Community Housing Corporation's Sierra Bonita Mixed Use Affordable Housing (2010) and La Brea Affordable Housing (2013), Executive Director Robin Conerly

When asked about comfort and whether the architecture ever got in the way of living, client responses were overwhelmingly positive, but there was a recurring grumble about something very Californian: sunlight. Whether it meant that fruit needed to always be kept in the fridge so as not to spoil too quickly, or whether clothes were being bleached in the sun, or large windows caused temperature-control issues, the ever-present sun of Los Angeles is a blessing but also a curse. However, these discomforts are always at the expense of something the clients find more important instead: views, inside-outside relationships, or the magical moments of light entering the building. As Lawson was quoted in the *Los Angeles Times* the year she and Westen moved into

15. Pilar Viladas, "Family Planning," *The New York Times*, November 7, 2009.

Patrick Tighe Architecture, in collaboration
with John V. Mutlow Architects, rendering of
La Brea Affordable Housing, Los Angeles, 2013

Morphosis Architects, Venice III,
Los Angeles, 1986

their Moss-designed home: "The sunlight streaming in and moving around constantly changes the house, and makes you aware of all the processes of change around you…The house wakes you up."[16] The effect of space on one's consciousness is a reccurring theme for clients, one that ultimately sheds light on its importance of design on identity and well being.

While it can be argued that the individual clients of residential architecture are essential to successful and innovative work, it is also critically important to address the role of the public as user and client. Nobel Prize–winning economist Amartya Sen advocates "the recognition that identities are robustly plural and that the importance of one identity need not obliterate the importance of others."[17] This pluralistic approach to identity is one that has often been espoused for a community like Los Angeles, a city populated by a multitude of identities. Charles Jencks, in his 1993 book *Heteropolis: Los Angeles, the Riots and the Strange Beauty of Hetero-Architecture*, writes that "difference and heterogeneity exist at many levels and this pluralism is itself a major reason why people continue to be drawn to Los Angeles."[18]

This heterogeneity can also be traced through the many scales on which these architects' work impacts the city. Their residential projects range in size, reason, and budget, but all share the notion that design can contribute to better, happier living environments. The scales of intervention also range; from exterior canopies, to additions, to remodeling and renovations, to completely ground-up projects for both single, and

multifamily buildings. While on the one hand, the buildings can be seen as sculptural objects, the overall fabric in which they exist is crucial to their impact on the communities surrounding them. Sue Keintz, director of housing development at the Community Corporation of Santa Monica, spoke toward this point when asked about Daly Genik Architects' Tahiti Affordable Housing (2009):

> Context is everything. Good architecture is a context with the capacity to define communities, to add beauty, to contribute to an individual's sense of strength, well being, worth. Bad architecture is, well, bad for everyone.

Robin Conerly and Rose Olson of West Hollywood Community Housing Corporation also spoke to the importance of the visual impact a building can have on the community around it. As Conerly says:

> At the time we were beginning the process of Sierra Bonita, the urban designer, John Chase, was working from the city side to make this building a showpiece. Monument isn't the right word, but something special on the east side redevelopment area. They wanted a building that would attract attention to this particular area. There was a lot of vision behind Sierra Bonita and what that might do, and a lot has come to pass since the building was completed, there's been a huge influx of housing that is more centered around La Brea. The kind of transformation that was anticipated is starting to happen.

16. "Room at the Top," *Los Angeles Times* home edition, April 25, 1993, 34.

17. Amartya Sen, *Identity and Violence: The Illusion of Destiny* (New York: Norton, 2006), 19.

18. Charles Jencks, *Heteropolis: Los Angeles, the Riots and the Strange Beauty of Hetero-Architecture* (London: St. Martin's Press, 1993), 7.

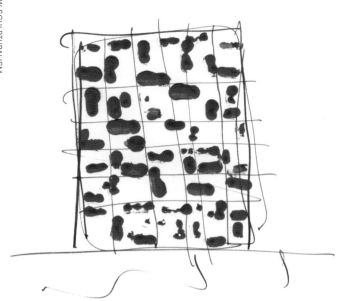

**Lorcan O'Herlihy Architects, drawing
for Formosa 1140, West Hollywood,
California, 2008**

Olson, director of housing, adds, "Los Angeles has many identities…
and it's a city that has been built once, but now it's going up, it's really
starting to become the second phase of what LA is going to be, and we
play a small part of that in terms of our pocket here in West Hollywood.
It's certainly gradual and evolving slowly, but just going up to five or six
stories, that's a different city." Just days earlier, Bergren, having lived in
her Morphosis home for more than twenty years, stood on her balcony
and looked over the roofscape of Venice before her and said, "I've
always enjoyed the on-the-roofs view and I know that one of these days
it will all be built up."

Each client brought an awareness of these changes, as well as a
firsthand understanding of the impact that architecture can have on the
individual, family, neighborhood, and city. As Marla Fiedler, a client of
Lorcan O'Herlihy Architects' multifamily project, Formosa 1140 (2008),
writes, "My building stands out from its surrounding. It's a piece of art
in an area that is developing, perhaps setting a tone for the neighborhood." What makes Los Angeles so unique is this perpetual movement
and change, a transformation that will only reaffirm its character as the
land of different and shifting identities, a place where a dream can come
true if one only "tries it." It is the attitude of clients like the ones inter-
viewed for this essay that helped shape so much of this city, an optimism
and openness to experiment, to embrace progress, and to accept and
trust creativity. One can only dream that many of these values continue
to be part of the conversations that will inevitably evolve into the future
scales of change in Southern California.

Hodgetts + Fung, Towell Library, University of California, Los Angeles, 1992

Left, top: Hodgetts + Fung, Towell Library, University of California, Los Angeles, 1992

Left, bottom: Hodgetts + Fung, Hyde Park Library, Los Angeles, 2004

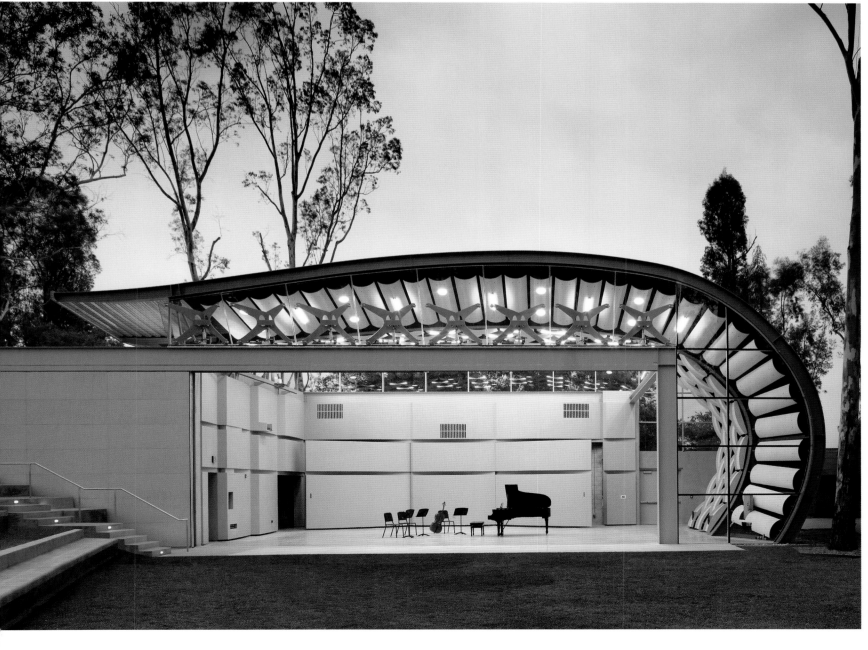

Left, top and bottom; and center: Randall Stout Architects, Steinhüde Sea Recreation Facility, Steinhüde, Germany, 2000

Right, top and bottom: Randall Stout Architects, Blair Graphics, Santa Monica, California, 2000

RANDALL STOUT ARCHITECTS

STUDIO WORKS ARCHITECTS

Left, top and bottom; and center, bottom: Studio Works Architects,
Pilibos School Library and Gymnasium, Los Angeles, 2006

Center, top; and right: Bestor Architecture, Floating Bungalow, Los Angeles, 2009

Left and center: Daly Genik Architects, Camino Nuevo Charter Academy, Los Angeles, 2000

Below: Daly Genik Architects, Art Center College of Design South Campus, Pasadena, California, 2004

DALY GENIK ARCHITECTS

Daly Genik Architects, Camino Nuevo High School, Los Angeles, 2006

Daly Genik Architects, Winnett, Santa Monica, California, 2007

Daly Genik Architects, Tahiti Affordable Housing, Santa Monica, California, 2009

Left, top: Lorcan O'Herlihy Architects, Formosa 1140, West Hollywood, California, 2008

Left, bottom: Lorcan O'Herlihy Architects, Willoughby 7917, West Hollywood, California, 2008

Center; and below: Lorcan O'Herlihy Architects, Habitat 825, West Hollywood, California, 2007

Left, bottom: Lorcan O'Herlihy Architects, Urban Paramount, Los Angeles, 2007

Left, top; and below: Lorcan O'Herlihy Architects, Flynn Mews House, Dublin, 2010

Left, top: Mark Mack Architects, Montalvo Art Studios, Saratoga, California, 1998

Left, bottom: Mark Mack Architects, Breitenleerstrasse Housing, Vienna, 1997

Center, top: Mark Mack Architects, Stremmel Residence, Reno, Nevada, 1992

Center, bottom: Mark Mack Architects, AB/BRO, Los Angeles, 2007

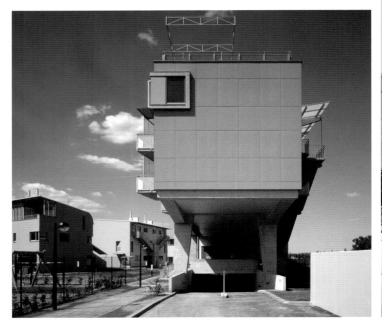

Right, top: Mark Mack Architects, Park Residence, Laguna Beach, California, 2009

Right, bottom: Mark Mack Architects, Frauengasse Housing, Judenburg, Austria, 2004

Michael Maltzan Architecture, Inner-City Arts, Los Angeles, 2008

Left, top and bottom; and center: Michael Maltzan Architecture, Ministructure No. 16, Jinhua, China, 2006

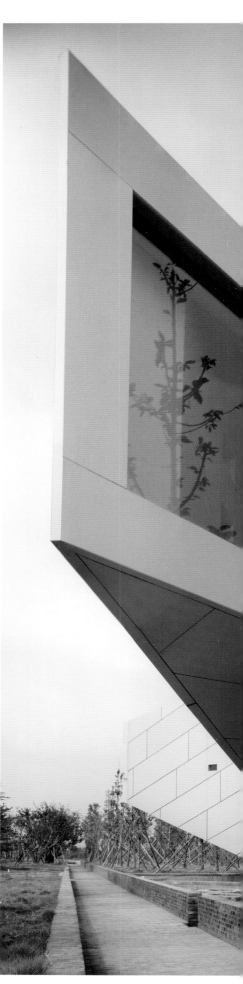

Right, top and bottom: Michael Maltzan Architecture, MoMA QNS, Long Island City, New York, 2002

MICHAEL MALTZAN ARCHITECTURE

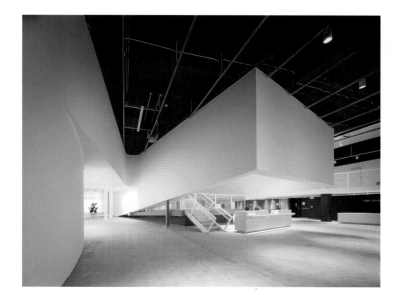

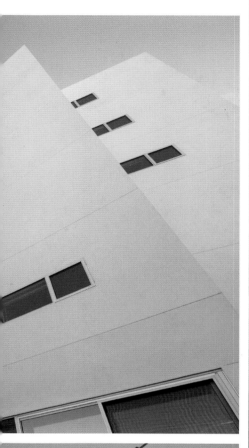

Left, top and bottom; and center: Michael Maltzan Architecture, Rainbow Apartments, Los Angeles, 2006

Right, top: Michael Maltzan Architecture, aerial view rendering of One Santa Fe, Los Angeles, 2014 (projected completion)

Right, bottom: Michael Maltzan Architecture, rendering of Star Apartments,
Los Angeles, 2013

Left, top and bottom: Neil M. Denari Architects, L.A. Eyeworks, Los Angeles, 2002

Center; and right: Neil M. Denari Architects, Alan-Voo House, Los Angeles, 2007

NEIL M. DENARI ARCHITECTS

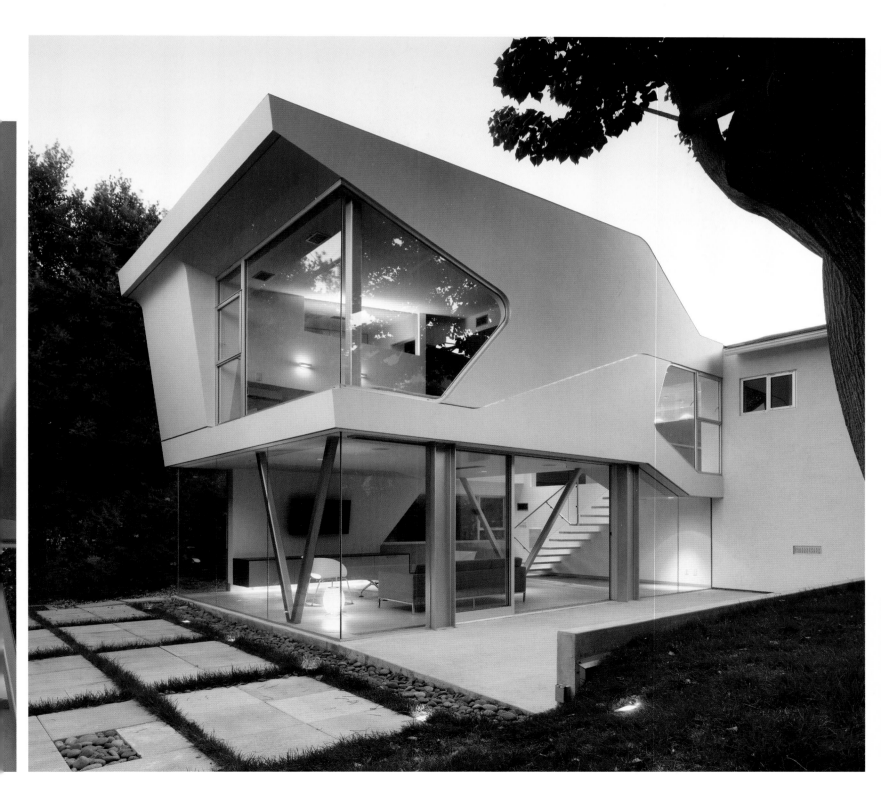

Belzberg Architects, Los Angeles Museum of the Holocaust, Los Angeles, 2010

BELZBERG ARCHITECTS

Below; and opposite, top left: XTEN Architecture, Sapphire Gallery, Los Angeles, 2009

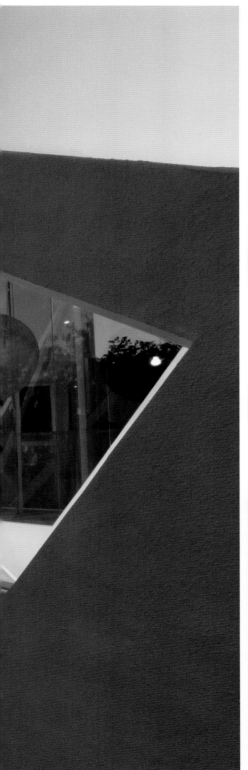

Left: Coscia Day Architecture and Design, Natalee Thai, Culver City, California, 2000

Center, top and bottom; and right: Coscia Day Architecture and Design,
Skywave House, Los Angeles, 2010

COSCIA DAY ARCHITECTURE AND DESIGN

Rebooting Reality
Sam Lubell

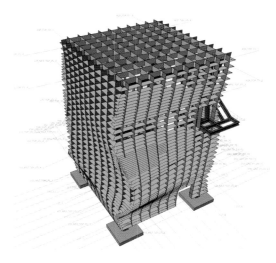

Eric Owen Moss Architects, parametric model of Hayden Tower, Culver City, California, 2007

Whatever its shortcomings, Los Angeles has always been a city of individuality, creativity, and vision. The city's architects specialize in dreams, resolving how to conquer the impossible and create something completely different. Just take a look at a Los Angeles hillside: few houses look the same. Or ask a local architect what his or her influences are: chances are the list will not be very long. The ambition to differentiate their work from that of others has always needed a medium, and technology has always been architects' most powerful tool. Luckily, technology, employed creatively, dominates Los Angeles' culture. It is in use at NASA's Jet Propulsion Laboratory at the California Institute of Technology (Caltech) in Pasadena, control center for the Mars rover; at aerospace, engineering, military, and boat design companies on the Westside; at tech start-ups near the beach; at Hollywood studios, creating digital animations and instantaneous sets; at theme parks, where miniature cities are designed and built to order; and at manufacturing plants that churn out computer-designed and -milled products. While these industries collaborate on occasion, generally their connections are informal. Ideas filter through casual conversation

Neil M. Denari Architects, HL23, New York, 2011

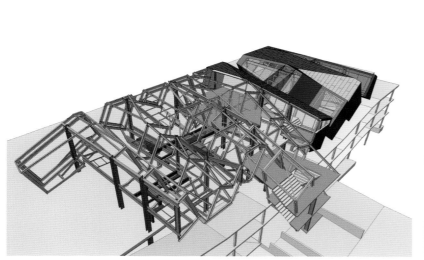

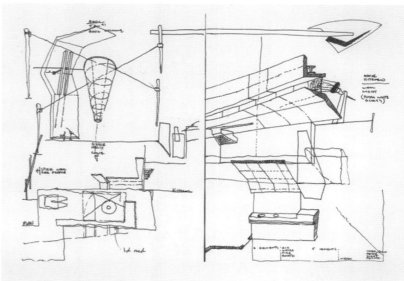

Eric Owen Moss Architects, parametric model of Pterodactyl, Los Angeles, 2013

RoTo Architects, sketch of Nicola Restaurant, Los Angeles, 1993

and spread through a willingness to try anything. They form a culture of technology-fueled risk taking that draws architects from across the country and the world.

The pulse of technology is also felt in what many consider to be the finest collection of architecture schools in the country: the University of Southern California (USC); the Southern California Institute of Architecture (SCI-Arc); the University of California, Los Angeles (UCLA); Cal Poly Pomona; and Woodbury University. Peripheral art and technology schools such as Caltech, Art Center College of Design, Otis College of Art and Design, Fashion Institute of Design and Merchandising, and the California Institute of the Arts (CalArts) funnel tremendous resources and talent into technological ingenuity. SCI-Arc has been focused on technology from the start; even its name, with the emphasis on the letters S-C-I, was a nod to the scientific process, points out school founder Ray Kappe.[1] Its first wave of professors, including Eric Owen Moss and Thom Mayne, explored new material technologies, researching unusual structural systems and ways to contort steel and glass; others, such as Kappe and Glen Howard Small, were interested in budding sustainability technologies, from solar panels to geothermal systems. Later tides, enabled by a fluid culture and loose hierarchy that has always promoted starting over, pushed further, questioning the modernist design strategies that the school had once taken for granted. Neil M. Denari carried the school into the early digital realm and Moss, who later became the school's director, took on faculty for whom advanced digital and materials research was a way of life. The school

emphatically shifted its focus to the infinite, overwhelming possibilities of digital technology, from visualization to, more recently, robotics and fabrication.

The legacy of Los Angeles' most renowned architects reads like a history lesson in technological innovation. Rudolph Schindler experimented with tilt-up concrete, which had been used primarily to construct industrial warehouses; Pierre Koenig, inspired by technical systems he studied in the military, partnered with Bethlehem Steel, hoping to create a new generation of lightweight, long-span steel houses; Raphael Soriano and Konrad Wachsmann tested the limits of prefabrication in steel and aluminum; John Lautner questioned formal and structural limits with his fantastic forms; and Anthony Lumsden and Cesar Pelli warped glass curtains and concrete and steel frames as if they were ribbon. Their brash descendants, led by Frank O. Gehry, Mayne, Moss, Michael Rotondi, and Craig Hodgetts, brought this technical counter-thinking to the mainstream, upending static forms and techniques that had been accepted as the norm for decades. Armed with analog tools, they warped walls, exploded floor plans, and tested new materials, eventually ushering their brand of sculpturalism into the digital realm and transforming expectations of what architecture could be.

Today's generation continues to differentiate itself through its use of technology. Three-dimensional modeling, revolutionary materials, and digital fabrication have replaced analog implements and crude digital ones, creating an architecture that is sleeker, more refined, and more

1. Ray Kappe, conversation with the author, September 21, 2012.

**Morphosis Architects, rendering of
Phare Tower atrium, Paris, 2017
(projected completion)**

could you write a two-dimensional plan for a scheme that fractures at every level and in every dimension? These architects developed forms and material variations that were so complicated that nobody, including them, knew how to build them. They gave contractors fits, and fights broke out on construction sites over what to do. Glass shattered in the process of being bent, and builders referred to physical models on site for direction. As Moss put it, his goal was, and still is, "proposing operations for which there is no technical precedent." Or, more simply: "We were interested in the exploration."[2]

Many of the transformations in form, material, and process came through trial, error, and persistence. A famous breakthrough occurred at Gehry's office in the early 1990s. Hoping to model some of its unusual shapes digitally, the firm partnered with IBM and aerospace consultant C-Cubed to use CATIA (Computer Aided Three-Dimensional Interactive Application), commercial software that had been employed mostly in the aerospace and automobile industries. Gehry's first physical manifestation using the CATIA application was the Barcelona Fish (1992), for which three-dimensional digital models helped contractors and steel manufacturers fashion complex physical geometries. The partition between design and manufacture, and between the two-dimensional and three-dimensional worlds, had begun to erode. "It was a tremendous risk," says Dennis Shelden, chief officer of Gehry Technologies, a software and consulting company that later spun off from Gehry Partners. "It violated the rules of how things were made."[3] Soon other firms were investigating similar digital techniques, propelling the Los

complex. For many, the biggest challenge is reality. Technologies have become so advanced that achieving true originality has become more difficult, while builders do not really know (or want to know) what to do with them. Many of today's trailblazers have steeped themselves in methods and materials that still may be decades away, if they ever come to fruition, and so they risk irrelevance in the built world even as they gain praise in small circles and lay the groundwork for future generations.

Barging Into the Digital World
Los Angeles' visionaries took a giant leap forward in the 1980s and 90s, their designs and techniques seizing the attention of the world and upending the technological status quo. From the beginning the anarchic forms of Gehry, Mayne, and their confederates reflected the chaos of contemporary (and Southern California) life, exuded a Pop art cheekiness, and reflected their makers' bad-boy personae, but they also reflected a desire to shatter the typical blueprint via technology. How

2. Eric Owen Moss, conversation with the author, August 28, 2012.   **3.** Dennis Shelden, conversation with the author, August 28, 2012.

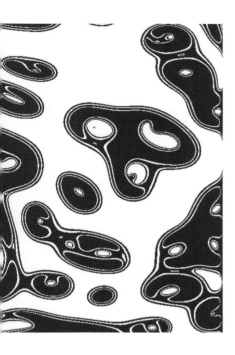

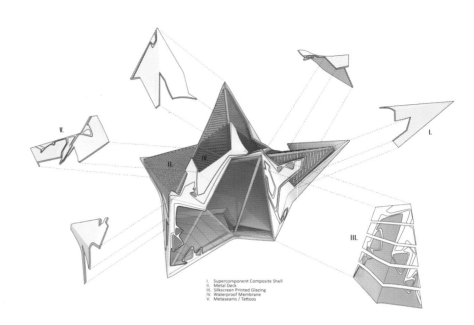

Tom Wiscombe Design, tattoo study of
Busan Opera House, Busan, Korea, 2010

Tom Wiscombe Design, diagram of Lo
Monaco House, Lugano, Switzerland, 2012

I.   Supercomponent Composite Shell
II. Metal Deck
III. Silkscreen Printed Glazing
IV. Waterproof Membrane
V.   Metaseams / Tattoos

Angeles scene like a rocket and transforming radicals' crazy ideas into reality. "It became obvious that this was the future," says Mayne, whose first digital project was the Diamond Ranch High School in Pomona, California, completed in 1996. "It was all or nothing. We could finally rationalize and simplify these things we had been working on."[4]

Fast-forward to the present, to a new breed similarly obsessed with splintering the norms of architecture. The result is, again, a body of research and creativity that makes Los Angeles one of the world's great architectural mixing bowls. The digital technologies now in use have advanced at a phenomenally fast pace. Primitive digital drawings and old-school sketches and models have been replaced by parametric modeling, digital optimization, new materials, and computer-controlled production. Processes that took Mayne and Moss years to perfect can now be carried out in a matter of days, and those rough, jagged forms that often came as a result of chaos now possess a level of refinement and precision that the digital pioneers could never have achieved, even if they had wanted to. Bewitching representations of the physical, often exhibiting complex geometries, are laid out on-screen, visualized in their totality, shared, and even manipulated in real time using modeling and visualization software like Rhino, 3ds Max, and Maya. A building with hundreds of pieces was once a nightmare to represent in two dimensions. Now such representations make sense. Algorithmic tools automate the design process, resolving challenges from solar exposure to formal resolution. Building-management tools like Revit and Gehry Technologies' G-Team organize work flow, allowing architects,

contractors, and engineers to share the same three-dimensional documents.

Models can be created digitally in a day, allowing designers' iterative process of trial and error to play out in a fraction of the time it once took. Composite materials, still little used in architecture, but increasing in popularity, increase strength, lightness, malleability, and translucency and replace small pieces with singular constructions. Varied and intricate parts and pieces can be shaped via digital fabrication, a process that has existed in manufacturing for years but is still in its infancy in architecture. It is already making an outsize impact. For example, Los Angeles specialist Andreas Froech, who uses laser cutters and gigantic robotic mills the size of automobiles (some were originally used in car factories), counts as clients many of Los Angeles' new cadre of experimental architects, including Greg Lynn FORM, Daly Genik Architects, Predock Frane Architects, Tom Wiscombe Design, JOHNSTONMARKLEE, and Patrick Tighe Architecture. Froech's customized components, pierced and shaved out of metal, wood, fiberglass, and foam, could not be formed by hand—they would require days of labor and provide considerably less precision.

Standing Out
Ironically, such technological advances can make inventiveness harder to achieve. How do you pioneer when making something amazing can come about relatively easily? How do you break away from a refined electronic tool that gives you so much power—at least virtually—but

4. Thom Mayne, conversation with the author, August 27, 2012.

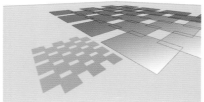

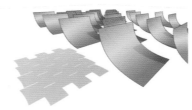

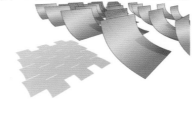

FreelandBuck, interior of Earl's Gourmet Grub, Los Angeles, 2010

DO | SU Studio Architecture, in collaboration with WROAD and Nous Consulting, diagram for *Bloom*, installation at Materials & Applications, Los Angeles, 2011

Atelier Manferdini, *Merletti*, installation at SCI-Arc, Los Angeles, 2008

at the end of the day starts to make your work predictable? Across the world, and not just in Los Angeles, projects have begun to look too slick, too digital, too accurate, too familiar. The temptations of form, surface, and blogworthiness have begun to trump other concerns. As Moss put it, "What was rare has become much more common. So now what?"

Originality comes from using digital tools in new ways or, in some cases, leaving them behind. Ben Ball, principal at Ball-Nogues Studio, calls this "misusing the technology." "There's an ideology built into the tool. If you abide by it, you will do things you've seen before,"[5] he said. His firm made its reputation by employing relatively untested parametric modeling software to devise complex installations made of hundreds of unique parts. At the time, they were a revelation, but now that such work has been displayed ad infinitum by a stream of young firms it has become, admitted Ball, "a bit of a cliché," and the firm is studying new approaches. For their 2012 SCI-Arc gallery installation *Yevrus 1, Negative Impression*, Ball-Nogues "misused" scanning tools typically operated by engineers, surveyors, and historic preservationists, cataloging physical objects such as a Volkswagen Beetle and re-creating them with huge, computer-fabricated molds into forms made out of sprayed-on paper pulp. "So much is generated purely in the digital world, so we decided to borrow from the physical world instead," said Ball. Much of his firm's work combines digital and analog construction, from the sprayed pulp to old-fashioned knitting. "Not all problems can be solved with digital tools," said Ball, who learned about employing whatever works best in designing sets for movies like *The Matrix* (1999) during an early stint in Hollywood set design.

Another pioneer in bending the digital rules is Tom Wiscombe, who, like many of his colleagues, has an office in his home and relies more on computers than on physical space. His current fixation is creating intriguingly different digital designs (which he calls "tattoos") by shuffling between hand drawings in Adobe Illustrator, computer models in Maya, and hybrid forms in ZBrush, a software used by Hollywood animators and costume makers to create forms and textures. "Certain bodies of work can be attributed to three scripts," explained Wiscombe. "I want to make things more mysterious and magical. I want to make it so you don't see the technology."[6] He is also exploring new composites, which he digitally molds and employs to create continuous structures with few (if any) seams or joints. One such construction is still hanging inside SCI-Arc, extending from a mezzanine as if it were a large insect. Fiberglass sandwich boards until recently were not kosher in construction, but their improved fireproof ratings and lowered costs are changing that. A home he is building in Lugano, Switzerland, will employ these digital and material technologies, highlighted by a star-shaped, fiberglass-shelled living space that appears to have crash-landed onto a more traditional steel-framed structure.

Wiscombe, who also teaches at SCI-Arc, typifies a generation of post-digital dreamers, aggressively reaching to create something distinct (and profound, and, perhaps, built, which is the real challenge) in an era when simply using advanced processes is not enough. Most split their time between academia and practice, carving out new directions as the cyber world merges with the material one. Los Angeles and New York

---

5. Ben Ball, conversation with the author, September 5, 2012. Further quotes are from this conversation.

6. Tom Wiscombe, conversation with the author, August 27, 2012. Further quotes are from this conversation.

Amorphis, *Go Figure*, installation at SCI-Arc,
Los Angeles, 2012

Greg Lynn FORM, prototype robot for
Revolving House, 2012

firm FreelandBuck, for instance, likes to misuse conventional building techniques through digital arrangement and assembly. The twisting wood baffles of its Earl's Gourmet Grub eatery (2010) do not really twist: they were asymmetrically laid out through parametric manipulation. A CNC-milled plywood mural explores gradient variation and the interplay of two-dimensional print and three-dimensional relief. Digital technology, in this case, is not a facilitator of form, but a means of adding new dimensions and variables to what is expected. The futuristic, cinematic, and alien digital images of Hernan Diaz Alonso—not to mention his built installations, with their hyperrealistic liquidity and shimmering, textured surfaces—have brought digital modeling to a hypnotic new level. Exploring sensation and randomness Jason Payne fitted his *Raspberry Fields* installation (2011) with a skin made of shingles that were intentionally attached incorrectly, producing an unpredictable curling pattern. Recent installations by Oyler Wu Collaborative combine incredibly complex digital modeling and production with decidedly low-tech, repetitive installation techniques. Doris Sung, in collaboration with Ingalill Wahlroos-Ritter and Matthew Melnyk, experiments with thermal bimetals that bend according to temperature, enabling their installation *Bloom* (2011) to open when the sun comes out. Elena Manferdini creates gorgeous installations and interiors, bridging computer fabrication with haute couture through intricate weaving, patterning, and folding.

The godfather of such computer-based material and fabrication research is Greg Lynn. He fled the digitally obsessed confines of Bernard Tschumi's Columbia Graduate School of Architecture for UCLA in the

1990s (and was subsequently followed by a horde of East Coast talent), exhilarated by a place "crawling with creative energy" that has "an intellectual curiosity about technology that doesn't exist elsewhere."[7] Since his arrival, he has been consumed with the intersection of design and manufacturing, which, to this day, remains the barely exploited holy grail of architecture. He has created scores of installations, many exploring the biomorphic integration of structure and form, with tools including digital production, new composites, and techniques gleaned from industrial manufacturers, set designers, and even boat-makers. His most recent work, an egg-shaped edifice that can be swiveled on its axis to instantaneously change its program, is being built at his studio with CNC molds, thermoforming, vacuum forming, and fiberglass. He is also designing a racing sailboat out of lightweight composites, utilizing not only fluid dynamics software from the nautical industry but finite element analysis software employed by engineers to test material qualities over every inch of a structure. While many of these technologies—including a CNC-molded fiberglass chandelier, laser-cut plywood framing, thermoformed kitchen and bathroom surfaces, CNC-milled beds and side tables, and digitally manipulated tiles—came together in his Bloom House (2010), this project is the exception to Lynn's work, not the rule. Asked if his pursuits are years ahead of their ability to be constructed, he replied, "That's really my job. That's what I do." While he hopes to construct more buildings, Lynn says his primary role is testing the future. Some, he notes, need to lead this purely experimental realm, and for him it is more energizing to work with BMW or Boeing than to work in what he calls the "servile" relationship of architectural

7. Greg Lynn, conversation with the author, September 6, 2012.
Further quotes are from this conversation.

Patrick Tighe Architecture, in collaboration with composer Ken Ueno and fabricator Machineous, *Out of Memory*, installation at SCI-Arc, Los Angeles, 2011

Patrick Tighe Architecture, rendering of Villa Skhirat, Skhirat, Morocco, 2014 (projected completion)

like Sucker Punch can get the word (or, more appropriately, the images) out instantaneously, regardless of whether it is a built project and whether there is anything in particular to say about it? So many of the most compelling images coming out of Los Angeles these days involve not new buildings, but installations from the SCI-Arc gallery, which was started in 2002 "in search of the perpetual experiment," as SCI-Arc director Moss put it.[8] Wiscombe, Ball-Nogues, Lynn, and virtually every significant talent in the city have had a turn. There, the slick digital world is moving to the more tactile physical one, albeit in a limited way. Other Los Angeles–area venues that always draw crowds include Materials & Applications in Silver Lake, WUHO Gallery in Hollywood, and MOCA at the Pacific Design Center in West Hollywood.

Ball, whose firm has become the archetypal art-installation designer, does not claim to be an architect at all. He regards much of his work as art that probes architectural questions and admits to struggling with how to define himself. "People don't like you jumping professions," he noted. Perhaps he is part of a new wave of designers that are at least partially involved with an architecture field that is quickly merging with installation art, set design, product design, video game design, and other creative pursuits, whether the profession likes it or not. In fact, many trained architects are jumping right into those professions out of school.

Builder-Innovators

Many of Los Angeles' new generation say they are stockpiling the lessons of experimentation in order to build, to scale up from experiment

patronage. "I'm not even sure any of this stuff will ever be standard practice in architecture," he admitted. "But I bet it will be in some form."

And he is not alone. Following the likes of Lynn (a major force at UCLA and in the city in general), Diaz Alonso (who directs SCI-Arc's graduate studies department), and Ball-Nogues Studio (which has created dozens of installations across the country), and seduced by powerful technology, many of today's young architects feel less pressure to build something. Why would you want to enter the heartbreaking, ugly world of construction when digital models, installations, and slick competition entries can be so damn impressive? When Facebook, Twitter, and blogs

8. SCI-Arc Gallery 2002–10, SCI-Arc Press, 2010.

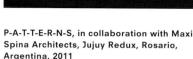

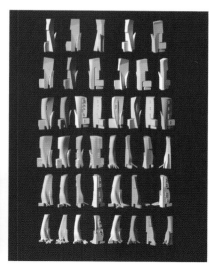

P-A-T-T-E-R-N-S, Zhixin Hybrid Modern Office Building, Chengdu, China, 2010

P-A-T-T-E-R-N-S, Prism Gallery, West Hollywood, California, 2009

P-A-T-T-E-R-N-S, in collaboration with Maxi Spina Architects, Jujuy Redux, Rosario, Argentina, 2011

Morphosis Architects, mockettes for Phare Tower, Paris, 2017 (projected completion)

to practice, but the biggest problem is getting the opportunity. Many complain that the infamously traditional (read: backward) and behemoth construction industry has not caught up to them, and that the tepid economy makes any work, let alone pioneering work, almost impossible. The youngest are, of course, just getting established. They add that Los Angeles, once a center for built innovation, just is not like that anymore. Much of the ingenuity, at least for now, is in ideas.

Wiscombe calls such unconventional experimentation "a long-term investment," recalling that it took visionaries like Le Corbusier decades to pull off some of their more revolutionary ideas. "I want to make a difference in the world and not be holed up in academia." His strategy includes collaborating with manufacturers, developing expertise on advanced software and materials, and pressuring builders to take him seriously. "Someone has to lay the groundwork. It can be painful at first." The architect is finally on his way with his new house, which, if completed, will add a built work to his trophy case of installations and never-built competition wins. Other builder-researchers are equally determined to make their mark by creating change in the built world, despite its cruel realities. Because the city's academic discourse is so strong, and so *loud*, some of these architects, ironically, do not seem to gain the same attention as their research-first counterparts.

That does not bother Tighe, who, when you visit his office, likes to show off his projects but does not like to indulge in architectural discourse. His most recent built experiments include skinning a housing project on La

Brea Avenue in West Hollywood with curved and etched CNC aluminum panels. CNC-etched aluminum is usually kept flat, according to Froech, who is working with Tighe on the project. Tighe is also working on a branching, digitally fabricated steel structure upon which he will build a villa in the Middle East (also rare: fabrication is generally used for surface, not structure). He characterizes the effort to keep his advanced designs from being dumbed down by clients as a constant battle. He views his one installation, an experiment with digitally molded foam at SCI-Arc, as a welcome respite, providing "instant satisfaction."[9]

Tighe's colleague at SCI-Arc, Marcelo Spina, has engaged in installation work as well, including a construction at the SCI-Arc gallery and the school's next graduation pavilion. But he is wary of making it the focus of his practice. "There's a limit to how much you can experiment. At a certain point there's no friction to it. There's no effect on reality outside of itself."[10] His firm P-A-T-T-E-R-N-S has incorporated Spina's advanced material research into several built projects. They used thermoformed polycarbonate panels and parametric modeling to construct a kinetic facade with a twisting steel structure for the Prism Gallery (2009) in West Hollywood. They produced digitally fabricated wax molds to create the simultaneously gridded and sloped glass-fiber-reinforced concrete edges of their Zhixin Hybrid Modern Office Building (2010) in China. And they most recently used CNC-milled fiberglass molds to produce relatively cheap undulating concrete panels in their Jujuy Redux (2011) project in Argentina.

9. Patrick Tighe, conversation with the author, August 28, 2012.

10. Marcelo Spina, conversation with the author, September 11, 2012.

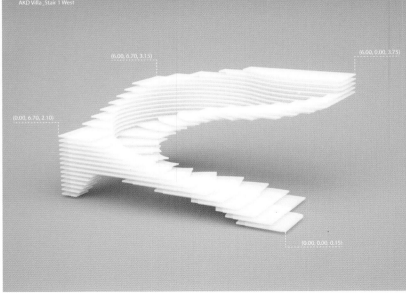

**Morphosis Architects, rendering of Perot
Museum of Nature and Science, Dallas, 2013**

**XTEN Architecture, digital staircase model
for Muscat Villa, Muscat, Oman, 2012**

The experimenters who are building *buildings*—from masters like Gehry, Mayne, and Moss, who are now some of the city's most prominent constructors, not its faraway dreamers—to youngsters (always a relative term in architecture) like Wiscombe and Spina, who are incorporating the most advanced academic research into built forms, are all, like their academic counterparts, struggling to push digital tools beyond the predictable.

Mayne is battling the sameness of digitally produced forms through complexity and tactility. His Phare Tower (opening in 2017) in Paris is composed of thousands of individualized units, each parametrically created and calibrated to respond to its environment. His Perot Museum of Nature and Science (2013) is contoured with rippling computer-fabricated concrete and steel walls. Neil M. Denari, who only began building at forty and now seems determined to break away from the world that he calls "technology as a career path,"[11] recently completed HL23 (2011), one of New York's most striking buildings. It implements meandering graphic parts that were built, stamped, bent, and laminated via digital fabrication, but were installed by hand. Michael Maltzan's recent innovations, embedded into ambitious projects like the Saint Petersburg Pier in Florida (under construction) and Playa Vista Park (2010) in Los Angeles, stem from merging architecture with landscape and engineering; he is hungrily exploring technologies in both those fields.

And if you squint, you can almost see the built works of the younger generation perched inside the SCI-Arc gallery. Spina's fluid concrete,

glass, and steel Residence (2009) in Argentina bears a striking resemblance to *The Element*, an undulating plastic installation he displayed at SCI-Arc in 2005. The massing of Wiscombe's house in Switzerland echoes his biomorphic *Dragonfly* installation from 2007. Austin Kelly of XTEN Architecture is creating a three-dimensional, digitally fabricated, and tessellated sculpture, but it will be realized as a staircase in a home in Oman. The winding rope and fabric surfaces of Oyler Wu Collaborative's Taipei high-rise sales center reflect the meandering surfaces of their SCI-Arc graduation pavilion *Centerstage* and their *Screenplay* installation (both 2012). The high-rise itself, with its relentless interplay of layered stainless steel mesh, fritted glass and steel panels, is a reflection of several other firm exhibits. And Murmur's Vortex House (2013), shaped like its geologic surroundings in Malibu, moves a lot like firm principal Heather Roberge's free-flowing installations at UCLA and Ohio State University.

But however advanced, unlike their academic-focused colleagues, these inventors are burdened with the realities of…reality. A building never looks as beautiful or functions as well as a rendering or an installation. Corners must be cut. Budgets must be met. Time ticks. Clients will not green-light everything, no matter how diligently they are lobbied. Some ideas just cannot be built yet. Concrete is not as light as it looks in graphics. And despite digital modeling and assembly, most construction techniques are essentially the same as they have been for centuries. If the work were as perfect and as advanced as an installation it would not be realized. This explains why academic experiment is so popular and important, and, on the other hand, why built experiment is equally vital.

11. Neil Denari, conversation with the author, August 14, 2012.

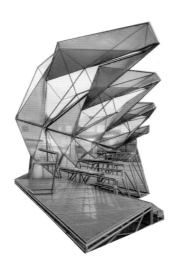

Oyler Wu Collaborative, rendering of Taipei Tower, Taipei, Taiwan, 2011

Oyler Wu Collaborative, *Centerstage*, installation at SCI-Arc Graduation Pavilion, Los Angeles, 2012

Murmur, rendering of Vortex House, Malibu, California, 2013

This divide between creative builders and researchers has always existed. Rudolph Schindler preferred construction as experiment; Konrad Wachsmann preferred designing prefab systems. Both had profound impact. But until recently the divide was weighted in favor of the builders. Now, thanks largely to technology, the opposite is true. Researchers' and inventors' obsession with the new will always be the heart of Los Angeles architecture, whatever form it takes. The city's thinkers are laying the ground for the field's future, moving us far beyond the complacency and unoriginality that dominates much of the profession and much more of the built world. But perhaps the Los Angeles urge to be different has reached its limit. Perhaps a few more dreamers need to step out of their digitally fabricated cocoons and further refine technologies and techniques that can be built today, that can bridge the gap between the studio and the site. Los Angeles continues to be a capital for architectural energy and invention, but whether it will once again be a capital of built work remains to be seen. Whether that even matters remains to be seen as well.

Brooks + Scarpa Architects, Bergamot Artist Lofts, Santa Monica, California, 1999

Left, top and bottom: Brooks + Scarpa Architects, Orange Grove, West Hollywood, California, 2004

Left; and center, bottom: Warren Techentin Architecture, Los Feliz Residence 1, Los Angeles, 2008

Center, top; and right: Warren Techentin Architecture,
Montrose Duplex, Montrose, California, 2010

WARREN TECHENTIN ARCHITECTURE

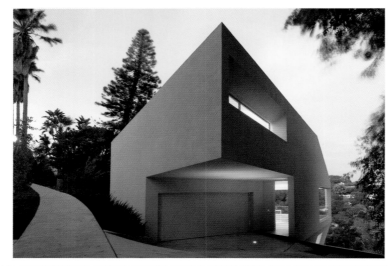

JOHNSTONMARKLEE, in collaboration with Diego Arraigada Arquitecto,
View House, Rosario, Argentina, 2009

Touraine Richmond Architects, One Window House, Los Angeles, 2005

Left: Patrick Tighe Architecture, Ashcroft Writer's Studio,
West Hollywood, California, 2007

Center: Patrick Tighe Architecture, Sierra Bonita Mixed Use
Affordable Housing, West Hollywood, California, 2010

Left, top: Patrick Tighe Architecture, Collins Gallery, West Hollywood, California, 2001

Left, bottom: Patrick Tighe Architecture, Live Oak Studio, Los Angeles, 2004

Greg Lynn FORM, in collaboration with Garofalo Architects and Michael McInturf Architects, Korean Presbyterian Church, Long Island City, New York, 1999

Greg Lynn FORM, SITE Santa Fe, New Mexico, 2012

AC Martin Partners, Hollenbeck Replacement Police Station, Los Angeles, 2009

Ball-Nogues Studio, *Maximilian's Schell*, installation at Materials & Applications, Los Angeles, 2005

Ball-Nogues Studio, *Feathered Edge*, installation at MOCA at the Pacific Design Center, West Hollywood, California, 2009

BALL-NOGUES STUDIO

Ball-Nogues Studio, *Table Cloth for the Courtyard at Schoenberg Hall,* installation at Herb Alpert School of Music, University of California, Los Angeles, 2010

Ball-Nogues Studio, *Liquid Sky*, installation at MoMA PS1 Contemporary Art Center, Long Island City, New York, 2007

Ball-Nogues Studio, *Yucca Crater*, installation near Twentynine Palms, California, 2011

Studio LA: The Tradition of Diversity
Nicholas Olsberg

Rodney Walker, model for Case Study House 16 (1947) published in *Arts & Architecture* magazine, September 1946

Lloyd Wright, Wayfarers Chapel, Palos Verdes, California, 1951

Great local outbursts of invention, even at their most varied and radical, never come out of the blue. The ideas are grounded in a long pattern of response to distinctive local circumstance, and their forms are rooted in a distinctive local culture. Most adventures in Los Angeles architecture at the turn of the twenty-first century are the product of a studio society: a loose cluster of ateliers working at relatively small scales. It may look like a young and amorphous community, animated by people who have dropped into it from everywhere, finding in its apparently formless landscape a tolerant terrain to punctuate with new ideas. But these architects find common cause not in a definable school of thought or doctrine, but in a powerful local attitude that is empirical, skeptical of rhetoric, respectful of the commonplace, and open to whimsy. Their offices are workshops for new forms and new means rather than seminars for apprenticeship in an idea. It is serious work, but it is not solemn.[1]

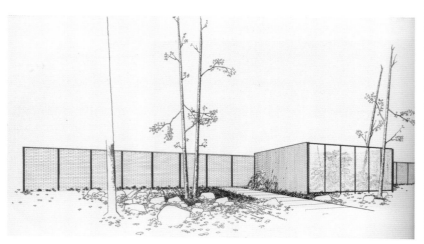

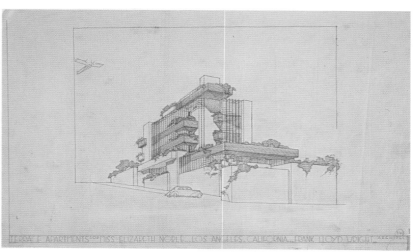

Craig Ellwood, drawing for Case Study House
#17, Beverly Hills, California (1956), published
in *Arts & Architecture* magazine, August 1954

Frank Lloyd Wright, perspective drawing for
Elizabeth Noble Apartments, Los Angeles,
1930 (project)

The Frank Lloyd Wright Foundation Archives, The
Museum of Modern Art | Avery Architectural & Fine
Arts Library, Columbia University, New York

Many of these features they owe to recent precedent: their sense of freedom in the examples of Frank O. Gehry, Michael Rotondi, Charles Moore, and others who came into view during the 1980s with work that lent credence to the informal and unexpected. Radically different from one another and radical in radically different ways, they scattered seemingly arbitrary, reminiscent, or playful new shapes about the city. It was not hard for these often flamboyant exercises to look almost tame in a city interspersed with far greater follies, from Watts Towers (1921–54) to the Tail o' the Pup (1946), the mechanistic Bradbury Building (1893) to the steamship (Pan-Pacific Auditorium) (1935), the Egyptomaniac Los Angeles Central Library (1926) to the Assyrian Samson Tire and Rubber Company (1930). Indeed, they appeared at the very moment when the status of such exuberant early landmarks, once ridiculed as Hollywood flamboyance, shifted from the despised to the much beloved, and from the meaningless to the instructive. Many were trained by those 1980s practices and stayed behind. Others have been drawn to Los Angeles because of its reputation for experimentation and the circumstances that have encouraged it—affordable studios, modest occasions to execute designs, and reasonable expectations of their being noticed. But there is a much longer course of circumstance from which this new tradition at its best derives.

Los Angeles was always a city fascinated by architecture, welcoming its varieties and tolerant of its fancies. It was a landscape built on the desire for a home of one's own. A vast sector of its economy, from the first housing boom of the 1880s to the crisis of 2008, has always been based around selling lots, building houses, and spinning the web of transport, services, media, and finance that sustains construction. Almost from the start, the city has sustained two parallel cultures of architecture: large-scale practices for public buildings, successively exemplified by such firms as Morgan and Walls, John C. Austin, John and Donald B. Parkinson, Albert C. Martin Sr., and William Pereira; and independent design ateliers, starting with the Pasadena School of the 1900s and continuing in most of the work we see in this volume. Many architects have moved from larger firms to found smaller ones, and many large firms have had their own moments of adventurousness—Morgan and Walls in Stiles Clements's time; Victor Gruen and Welton Becket in the late 1950s; and Pereira and Daniel Mann Johnson and Mendenhall, with their stables of avant-garde designers from Europe, in the 60s.

Within this creative history, however, there is a legendary or heroic epoch, what we might call a "studio era," dating from the late 1930s to the early 60s, when small ateliers flourished during the golden age of Hollywood. The work of that time is now so widely celebrated that, though far from ubiquitous on the ground, it serves as the inevitable backdrop against which the theater of new design is played. These studios spoke with dramatically varied voices and to very different effect. But there are some fundamental ideas and shared origins in their work that cast its immense variety in a common light. Many of those common features derived from the discomfiting figure of Frank Lloyd Wright, with whom so many architects in the region had worked and trained. They were centered on an approach to shaping space that

1. Much of the research for this study was developed between 2000 and 2003 as part of an exhibition project for the Cite de l'Architecture et de la Ville in Paris, initiated by Jean-Louis Cohen and since suspended.

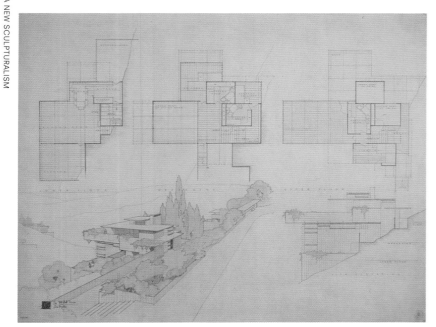

Frank Lloyd Wright, perspective drawing for
All Steel Housing Project, Los Angeles, 1937
(project)

The Frank Lloyd Wright Foundation Archives, The
Museum of Modern Art | Avery Architectural & Fine
Arts Library, Columbia University, New York

Harwell Hamilton Harris, bird's-eye
perspective drawing of Entenza House,
Los Angeles, 1937

Harwell Hamilton Harris Papers, The Alexander
Architectural Archive, The University of Texas
Libraries, The University of Texas at Austin

looked for unique solutions via the Wrightian procedure of making an uninhibited analysis of each unique situation. The result is a distinctive history of designs that, however individualistic, seem to be generated by a common desire to uncover an innate and peculiar economy in each purpose, site, and setting.

The Economy of Assembly: Frank Lloyd Wright, Richard Neutra, and Rudolph Schindler

For progressive Los Angeles architects during this studio era, there were a number of common lineages. Those who trained afar were typically linked not to the old-line Beaux Arts schools of the Northeast but to more liberal programs like that of Cornell University in Ithaca, New York (with its pioneering five-year curriculum, international perspective, and open enrollment of minorities and women), and the University of Michigan, Ann Arbor (aligned from 1923 onward with European modernism through Knud Lonberg-Holm and Eliel Saarinen). During the 1920s, forward-thinking graduates of the University of Southern California, talked sadly of the rigidity of the architecture faculty there. But the college's conservatism was readily offset by the city's numerous art schools, where such adventurous courses as Kem Weber's lectures on color theory were particularly influential.

Wright attempted to settle in Los Angeles after his return from Japan in the early 1920s, and his built work from that time—the Barnsdall complex and the four block houses—perhaps strives too hard to find an expressive new monumental order for a cityscape he deemed

cacophonous and insubstantial. Conjuring up some vague archaic moment lost to history, these houses are, however, brilliantly sited, imaginatively planned, and, in their plays of space and light, almost ecstatic advocates of what the shaping of a building can do to luxuriate in California's sunshine and vistas. More persuasive and markedly more modern are two unbuilt projects that followed. One, the Elizabeth Noble Apartments of 1929, proposes a vertical cluster of garden apartments. The other, an all-steel development for open land in the Baldwin Hills, strings separate dwelling units along a web of steel walkways, with parking in a common facility at the center of the tract. Each uses the idea of a monochromatic palette to balance a disorderly cityscape: the choice of concrete and glass in one case and steel and glass in the other emphasizes the geometric lines of the architecture, structuring the topography much more decisively than the crusty mullions of his earlier textured blocks. At the same time the challenge of reconciling privacy to community while still opening the dwellings to the outdoors and to light and vista makes the point that nothing in this shallow, horizontal city is ever really autonomous.

All these ideas are echoed and developed in the work of Rudolph Schindler and Richard Neutra, the most important of Wright's vast Los Angeles progeny and, through the schooling their short-lived joint practice provided to Harwell Hamilton Harris, Gregory Ain, and Raphael Soriano, the figures who did most to move Wright's ideas into the next generation. Both came to Wright after training in Vienna and worked with him for longer than they later claimed, Schindler for at least seven years in

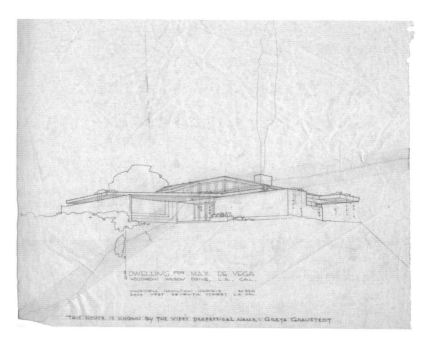

Harwell Hamilton Harris, perspective
drawing for Greta Granstedt House,
Los Angeles, 1938

Harwell Hamilton Harris Papers, Alexander
Architectural Archive, The University of Texas
Libraries, The University of Texas at Austin

Man Ray photograph of Harwell Hamilton
Harris's Cecil J. Birtcher Residence,
Los Angeles, 1942

Harwell Hamilton Harris Papers, Alexander
Architectural Archive, The University of Texas
Libraries, The University of Texas at Austin

Chicago and Los Angeles, and Neutra for shorter periods in Wisconsin and Los Angeles, from 1923 to perhaps 1928. Both filtered Wright's lessons through the lens of Otto Wagner and Adolf Loos, quickly moving on to produce work that looks superficially nothing like his own. But Wright's noble conversations between light and enclosure, levels and hillside, rooms and gardens are echoed in Neutra's Lovell House (1928) and the Jardinette Apartments (1927), a slowly evolving project in which Ain, Harris, Schindler, and Soriano were all initially involved. Inquiries into clustering small dwellings into colonies within the urban landscape not only dominated the mature work of Ain, Neutra, and Schindler in the 1930s, but became a vital force in establishing a regional approach to achieving scale through a sort of controlled dispersal in which perfectly compact solutions are reached by apparently scattering their parts.

Many of these early clustered systems followed the economic imperatives of the early bungalow court, in which owners of single lots constructed a colony of income-generating units around their own apartments. This was a wonderfully democratic regional typology that persisted well into the postwar era, produced a sense of living within a miniature campus, and (with a single resident client to satisfy rather than a developer) allowed extraordinary latitude to the imagination of the designer. These systems sowed the seeds for a much broader negotiation among autonomous spaces, shared structures, and a common landscape that marked the first municipal and defense department housing projects of 1939–44. Those social housing experiments blossomed in turn in the immediate postwar years as architects like Ain

and Whitney R. Smith, addressing the housing crisis of the city's population boom, configured original designs for cooperatives and speculators' tracts. Others, like John Lautner (another Wright apprentice) carried the same logic to the clustered school and workplace, interlocking small units within a larger frame. What emerges is a distinctive and very long Los Angeles tradition in which the same ideas of scale, compactness, and adjacency echo in the courtyard and garden dwellings of the 1910s and 20s as well as among the roadside commercial courtyards and school and office campuses that mark our own time.

The Economy of Space: Harwell Hamilton Harris
Neutra carried the same concerns with site into his study of single dwellings, becoming almost obsessively interested in how buildings fit into the larger landscape, often drawing sight, vista, vanishing points, and light lines round the whole 360 degrees of a location before settling on how to place and shape a structure. Among those who came after Neutra, Harris, an unabashed Wright admirer, and Lautner were equally fanatic about establishing site, particularly in regard to adjacencies, sunlight, and vista. Harris sometimes diagrammed the light and prospect in a single room throughout the day and over the seasons, while Lautner worked and reworked schemes in the Hollywood Hills to find plans that would at once screen the unsightly or intrusive and open to light and viewpoints. The result for both architects, especially as they took the roadway and approach by car into account, was often a building in total defiance of the conventions of presentation; it might be imperceptible from the road, drop off a slope, be shaped counter to the

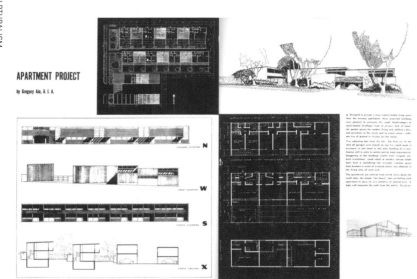

Gregory Ain, "Apartment Project," article
published in *Arts & Architecture* magazine,
March 1946

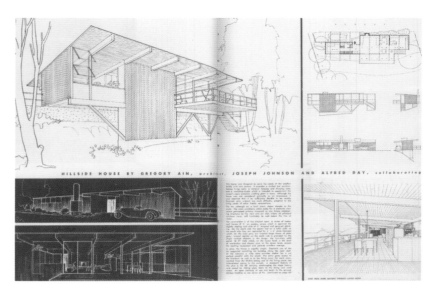

Gregory Ain, "Hillside House," article
published in *Arts & Architecture* magazine,
February 1950

aspect of its neighbors, or present only services, garage, and driveway
to the street. A very definite Los Angeles orthodoxy emerged in which
the building served not to announce its presence but only to keep its
occupants company.

Another emerging convention derived from the essential horizontality
of the California condition. Laying out a plan on a single floor with
access to gardens might now seem a perfectly obvious way to plan
a building in an expansive landscape, a warm climate, a city in which
mobility is paramount, and a society where the bungalow has already
been established as the basic housing type. But working complex,
unconventional, and increasingly open plans into bungalow forms on
compact sites called for a considerable leap in imagination, and the
Los Angeles of the 1930s, with its bachelor households, collaborative workshops, and experimental schools, demanded unorthodox
arrangements for living, work, and movement. Harris was especially
adept at varying and staggering spaces to achieve this. In the miniature
scale of his John Entenza House (1937), the whole scheme is simply a
platform moving from the narrowest anchor on the street to overhang
the canyon behind. His Greta Granstedt (1938) and Cecil J. Birtcher
Houses (1942), one on the slope of a hill and the other cresting it,
each splay out so that the wide vistas at their backs remain unfocused
and unframed. To achieve this, the roof becomes paramount in all
his work, shifting heights to vary the spaces underneath, lapping and
overhanging to manage the fall of light. While this clearly speaks to the
flamboyant rooflines of Pasadena's Craftsman architecture, it serves

the sober and less theatrical purpose of organizing and shaping with
light the space beneath.

The Economy of Means: Gregory Ain

Ain had experimented with low-cost housing in his Dunsmuir Flats of
1937, but his clustered dwellings of the postwar era show an even
more remarkable virtuosity of the inevitable, as he adapted his notion
of the open plan and its economy to different sites and densities. He
was equally ingenious in establishing a graphic language for publication
that made their pragmatic virtues extraordinarily clear and matched
that to a rigorously analytic text. A 1950 proposal for a hillside house,
for example, is replete with references to simplicity, economy, and
the carving out of private space "designed to serve the needs of the
smallest family unit—one person." The construction—timber beams and
slabs—"is of the simplest type"; the plan "is equally simple," with the
shelf of the roadway used to provide a level parking space, eaves doing
double duty as shelter and carport, furnishings incorporated into walls,
and living space divided by storage partitions. Moving the building
out over the canyon on a single plane, Ain certified that the "same
conditions which make for a dramatic view assure permanent privacy,
inasmuch as any future neighboring structures…will inevitably be well
below the line of vision."[2]

The resulting house reads, in rectilinear form and in wood, almost iden-
tically to Harris's Entenza House, placed in curved concrete on a similar
hillside fifteen years before. There is much logic and little magic in these

2. Gregory Ain, "House by Gregory Ain," *Arts & Architecture* 67,
no. 2 (February 1950): 27–28.

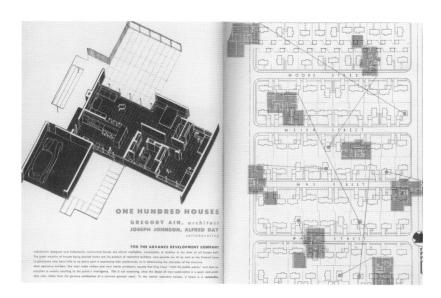

Gregory Ain, "One Hundred Houses,"
article published in *Arts & Architecture*
magazine, May 1948

Lloyd Wright, Wayfarers Chapel,
Palos Verdes, California, 1951

words, but the diagrammatic clarity of Ain's drawings cannot conceal the underlying lyricism. The gentle abstraction of sunlight and topography through suggested outline, partial lines, and spots; the rendering of decisive structure against uncertain landscape; the ability to show perspective without shadows: all speak to a romance with the ground, the sun, and how forms might be shaped to suit them.

Los Angeles at Midcentury: The City as Case Study

Ain's proposals for collective housing projects appeared in issue after issue of John Entenza's Los Angeles–based *Arts & Architecture* magazine as one set of solutions to the postwar housing crisis. The better-known Case Study House program initiated by the magazine and addressing a wider range of household incomes was another. It is the steel and glass Case Study projects of Charles and Ray Eames, Craig Ellwood, Soriano, and Pierre Koenig, none appearing before 1949, which are best remembered. But it was Schindler's apprentice, the artist Rodney Walker who dominated the early phase, with informal structures framed in wood clearly bearing the hallmarks of Schindler and Wright.

Indeed, architecture in Los Angeles had never lain in obscurity. As early as 1904, a compendium featuring projects by Morgan and Walls, A. Wesley Eager, Sumner Hunt, and John Parkinson had appeared;[3] annual exhibitions of the LA Architectural Club (later the city's American Institute of Architects chapter) began in 1907, and were extensively published in its yearbook. National and regional architectural magazines looked at new work in Los Angeles throughout the 1920s. Wright's

Los Angeles work—built and projected—was the primary source of illustration for his essays "Creative Matter in the Nature of Materials," widely read in America, and for the important Wright monographs that appeared in Holland, Germany, and France in the years 1925–28.[4] Neutra's innovations were never out of sight in the 1930s, and Soriano's projects took a special place in *Architectural Forum*'s "100 Houses" of 1938. Ain's Dunsmuir Flats appeared before the war in journals around the world, and long before Entenza took over *Arts and Architecture*, adventurous new work from Los Angeles was appearing in that California journal.

From 1944 onward, as architectural journals, exhibitions, and popular magazines focused on what the new domestic landscape of a postwar world might look like, Los Angeles moved from architectural curiosity to case study for the future. In just a few months between the end of 1949 and the summer of 1950, Neutra appeared on the cover of *Time*;[5] *Holiday* magazine published a special issue on the Southern California lifestyle (focusing on Lautner);[6] and a demonstration house by Ain took over the garden of New York's Museum of Modern Art. Meanwhile, large-scale local exhibitions, such as Scripps College's "Sixteen Architects" (1950), and the pioneering photographic *A Guide to Contemporary Architecture in Southern California* in 1951 broadcast the importance of contemporary work in Los Angeles in the culture of the region itself, drawing attention to its variety. By 1956 the movement was celebrated enough to justify an exhibition locating its regional roots.

3. See J. L. LeBerthon, *Our Architecture: Morgan & Walls, John Parkinson, Hunt & Eager* (Los Angeles: J. L. LeBerthon, 1904).

4. See Frank Lloyd Wright's series of fourteen articles, collectively known as "Creative Matter in the Nature of Materials," for *Architectural Record*, beginning with "In the Cause of Architecture I: The Architect and the Machine," *Architectural Record* 61 (May 1927). See also See H. Th. Wijdeveld, *The Life-Work of the American Architect, Frank Lloyd Wright* (Amsterdam: C. A. Mees, 1925); H. de Fries, *Frank Lloyd Wright Aus dem Lebenswerke eines Architekten* (Berlin: Ernst Pollak, 1926); and *Frank Lloyd Wright* (Paris: Éditions Cahiers d'art, 1928).

5. See the cover of *Time* 54 (August 15, 1949) and the accompanying article "New Shells," 58–66.
6. See *Holiday* 7, no. 1 (January 1950).

"Blueprints for Modern Living: History
and Legacy of the Case Study Houses,"
installation at the Museum of Contemporary
Art, Los Angeles, Temporary Contemporary,
1990

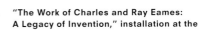

"The Work of Charles and Ray Eames:
A Legacy of Invention," installation at the
Vitra Design Museum, Weil am Rhein,
Germany, 1994

The eclectic and various character of the region's buildings had been noted from the start, with East Coast writers from the mid-1920s onward sometimes turning a skeptical eye toward its apparent futurism and flamboyance. But two MoMA survey exhibitions titled "Built in the U.S.A." seemed to take that variety for granted and locate the inherent unity within it.[7] The first show, in 1944, looked back on forty-seven works made since the museum's 1932 International Exhibition, finding by far the largest number (more than a quarter) in California, with Ain, Harris, Neutra, and Soriano all appearing in works that spoke to social needs and economies of scale and construction. Of the forty-three works in Philip Johnson's 1953 version of the exhibition, as many as seven were Southern California projects from the immediate postwar years, with houses by Ain, Harris, Neutra, and Soriano appearing alongside Maynard Lyndon's Vista Elementary School (1950), the Eameses' Case Study House No. 8 (1949), and Lloyd Wright's Wayfarers Chapel (1951). Each of these signally modern projects is dominated by the building's relationship to landscape, light, vista, and passage between indoors and out. In the context of Wayfarers Chapel, this motley assortment of buildings in different materials, palettes, and settings begins to show a surprising amount in common. Frank Lloyd Wright's oldest son used a slightly raised platform, shallow baseline, reflective surfaces, wooden arch, and vegetated vistas, along with a totally unorthodox imbalance between shelter and transparency, reflecting his forty years of practice in Southern California. These ideas are echoed in each of the other projects shown: the shapes of Harris's Ralph Johnson House (1951), the Eameses' photography and film of

their studio home, Neutra's plan for the Warren Tremaine House (1950), Lyndon's arrangement of his school pavilions, and Soriano's siting of his 1950 Case Study House. It is odd perhaps that it was the much citified Johnson who discerned how the extraordinary variety of Los Angeles architecture united around these shared approaches to the local qualities of openness to light and landscape.

The Economy of Form: Raphael Soriano and Craig Ellwood

If Ain's representation of simplicity betrays some poetry beneath its analytic surface, there can be no doubt of the lyricism behind the ever more absolute simplification that appears in Soriano's work. Beginning with clear nods to his apprenticeship with Neutra, Soriano's prewar projects draw on the complicated language of Neutra's Lovell House, articulating elaborate relationships between members of white metal and the glass between them. But even in the 1930s, Soriano's portrayal of his interiors, in which rooms are shown as near voids, with nothing but a chair, a table, a shelf, and a house plant, pointed to a growing formal economy. By 1950 his drawings show very plainly what he was trying to achieve: a building that is nothing but the solid planes of its floor and roof and the transparent sheets of window wall. It is architecture composed of almost nothing except the views beyond it and the gardens they reveal.

Ellwood's pavilions seem to speak a similar language, but derive from quite contradictory intentions. For Soriano the building was a frame for the metaphysics of what surrounds it. For Ellwood, the building itself told

7. For information on the contents of each of these exhibitions at the Museum of Modern Art, see "Museum of Modern Art Selects Forty-Seven Buildings of Best Modern Design Built in U.S.A. Since 1932," MoMA press release from April 12, 1944, available at http://www.moma.org/docs/press_archives/930/ releases/MoMA_1944_0016_1944-04-12_44412-14.pdf?2010; and "'Built in U.S.A.: Post-War Architecture' to be Shown at Museum," MoMA press release from January 18, 1950, available at http://www.moma.org/docs/press_archives/1673/releases/ MOMA_1953_0003_3.pdf?2010.

"California Design, 1935–1960: 'Living in a
Modern Way,'" installation at the Los Angeles
County Museum of Art, Los Angeles, 2012

that metaphysical tale, using the landscape as a backdrop against which the natural poetry of structure can be felt. Soriano is about the absence of building. Ellwood is about its presence. Ellwood's approach—the way walls carry the visual argument of his drawings and the poetics of structure inform his verbal rhetoric—dates entirely from the postwar era. His intellectual genetics were very distant from Wright's, and his studio practice, like that of Gehry or Maltzan, successfully transitioned to the size and terms of full-scale public buildings. Like the Eameses, Ellwood was interesting not simply for what he did—finding ways to adapt universal structural and material ideas to the particulars of California— but by being the first truly famous Los Angeles architect, outdoing even Neutra in European monographs, exhibitions, statements, and interviews and cutting a particularly dashing figure. Staffed with students and associates of Ludwig Mies van der Rohe, his was the one experimental office tuned to the demands for monumental late modernism that, starting in the mid-1950s and ripening until the oil crisis of 1973, expressed Los Angeles' growing desire to start looking just like everywhere else.

The Economy of Structure: John Lautner
The high points of the postwar years were short lived. By 1955, Ain, Harris, and Soriano had left Los Angeles. A few years later, Rodney Walker retreated to run a restaurant in Ojai, California; Maynard Lyndon moved to Germany; Neutra was reestablished in Vienna; and newer lights such as Koenig and Ray Kappe were either out of work or had refashioned themselves as urban planners. The reemergence of lively studio practices during the early 1980s was thus more a revival of a

sleeping tradition than its continuation. One of the few survivors of the retreat to urban design and corporate architecture was Lautner, whose tiny practice continued to find the occasional inventive and wealthy client well into the 1970s. Lautner's was a plastic language grounded in a transcendental view of the natural world, in which relationships to vista, sunlight, and starlight are the primary objectives of each building. His means of achieving such relationships was to find a particular sheltering structural geometry that fit the site and its prospects. The result might look eccentric or fanciful at first glance, but seen from all sides—and especially from inside out—the logic behind the shape always appears. Two variations on the idea of the tent appear in the Chemosphere House (1960), perched high on a pole to gain an outlook on the San Fernando Valley, and the Midtown School (1960), whose cluster of lightweight wigwams floated on the soft landfill of a valley floor. Each employs different structural systems to open up strong sensations of light and the outside world. At the Dan Stevens House (1968) in Malibu, a pair of intersecting half arches creates within the narrow lot a great channel to the light on both the land and seaward sides. Just as Harris could eliminate the notion of front and back, or Ain and Soriano the idea of doorway and window, Lautner's curved forms eliminated the distinction between wall and roof, leaving the molded structure of a cave, shell, or hull to do the job of both.

Reviving the Native Tradition
Harris and Ain were natives of Los Angeles' outer edges, steeped in the more eccentric of the region's architectural traditions. Harris's family

Koning Eizenberg Architecture, Waterloo
Heights Apartments, Los Angeles, 2002

Koning Eizenberg Architecture, 5th Street
Family Housing, Santa Monica, California,
1998

were builders among the string of new health resorts and citrus-packing towns that opened along the railroad from Redlands to Pasadena; he recalled a boyhood watching new structures rise from virgin land as well as daily walks to school that awakened an abiding love for the barns, trellises, and stalls of the local ranchos, and for how that rough-hewn work was wedded to Asian echoes and to Progressive Era ideals of the "simple house." Ain grew up among the "Little Landers" of the Verdugo Valley, whose social doctrine was constructed around the idea of an absolute economy of scale and materials. Compact buildings of locally harvested river rock were an essential ideological feature of their utopian landscape.

Walker and Ellwood came to the region young and had quite another experience of Los Angeles. Walker was among the legion of art students in a city whose aerospace and entertainment industries had an insatiable appetite for draftsmen, designers, and photographers. Ellwood left high school during the war, becoming an army engineer and quickly allying himself with the city's first major industry, home building, upon his demobilization, opening a flourishing business as a contractor. But many more of the central figures of the studio era—Lloyd Wright from Chicago; Weber, Schindler, Davidson, Jock D. Peters, and Neutra from Germany and Austria; Lautner from upper Michigan—essentially came to Los Angeles with limited experience in order to open a practice or, like Soriano from the island of Rhodes, to train for one. The studio tradition has since been revived many times as Los Angeles has become a destination for architects, owing to the fortunate combination of an expansive

urban topography, open-minded clients, informal building practices, a forgiving climate, an aerospace industry constantly generating new materials and techniques, and a fondness for small-scale typologies.

What has changed, however, is the different attitude to the environment. Wright saw the city as an aesthetic wasteland. Garret Eckbo talked of his great landscape work as merely a counter to the appalling ugliness of the surroundings. Lautner found the city, dominated by bean fields, dirt roads, and oil derricks, so ugly that he was physically sickened. Sophisticates of the 1950s tended to see nothing but a deadly miasma of freeways and tract houses, while those of the 60s noticed only Johnny Carson's "beautiful downtown Burbank" or topographies of impending disaster, Disneyland banality, and rudely flamboyant modernity. Since then, however, respect for the built patterns and design traditions of the region has continued to grow alongside the conservancy movement, a rage for "midcentury modern," and a more and more admiring gaze on the work of Gill, Schindler, Neutra, and the postwar masters. The result has been careful restorations, critical studies, and revelatory exhibitions, along with real estate values that rise markedly on the strength of an architect's name, and minor monuments of design reconstructed as trophy dwellings for private parties. Los Angeles, for so long perceived as a disjointed wilderness of tracts and freeways, is now celebrated as a vast coherent map upon which myriad ingenious landmarks of design have happily fallen.

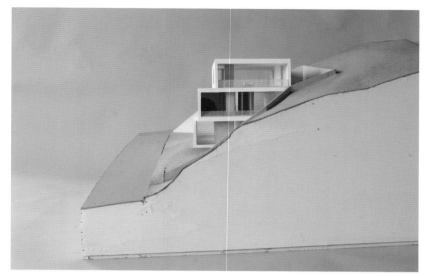

**Escher GuneWardena Architecture, model
for Sola/Wright Residence, Los Angeles,
2009**

A Cultural Economy of Architecture

We can see this new regard for the past reflected in the persistence of local traditions of invention in dramatically different contemporary practices. One of the most radically original voices among the studio architects emerging in 1980s Los Angeles has been the most instrumental in describing the legacy of the studio era. Hodgetts + Fung have designed, over three decades, landmark exhibitions on the Case Study House program and the Eameses (both of which they helped conceive), as well as on the flowering of California modern design. Their work has decisively captured the era's key dynamics: that the new design language was open to all consumers and that a better life would come from it. As we connect the molded geometries in the background of the Eameses' linear architecture to the molded form of Gehry's Vitra Design Museum (1990), we see how much of Los Angeles' design experiments in one time and scale have affected the architecture of another. Hodgetts + Fung takes no stylistic cues from the subjects of their exhibition designs and studies, but does share the Eameses' fundamental sense of an economy of design. All media are deemed expressive; no material useful in one context is spurned in another; no temporary structure is treated lightly; no reference to the past is improper; and no work is too ordinary or temporary for the ingenuity of design.

Nothing looks less like the work of Hodgetts + Fung than that of Koning Eizenberg Architecture, established by Australians Hank Koning and Julie Eizenberg in 1981 and closely associated with buildings for social groups on the margins of poverty or distress. They have an eye for the

historical palette, drawing on sometimes accidental aesthetic patterns and elements in the local landscape. In the Waterloo Heights Apartments (2002), their special-needs housing for the margins of Los Angeles' Silver Lake neighborhood, the designers picked up on residents' desire for reassuring echoes of the Arts and Crafts bungalow, adding the hurricane fences and corrugated plastic shelters typical of the area's blue-collar lawns and driveways. This vibrant bricolage of the found and the invented is grounded in the same approach to clustering (evident in 5th Street Family Housing [1998], their early mixed-income housing for Santa Monica) that Wright, Schindler, and Neutra launched in the 1920s. They then assemble the complex not from a profligate raid upon sources, but with an economic eye toward the most useful elements of both our well-designed and careless pasts.

Like Hodgetts + Fung, Escher GuneWardena Architecture looks to past and future and, like Koning Eizenberg Architecture, for an absolute economy of method and means. Frank Escher, Swiss-American, and Ravi GuneWardena, Sri Lankan-American, collaborate on restorations, artist installations, and freestanding projects, all informed by their closeness to Los Angeles' modern heritage. Their Sola/Wright Residence (2009) was built on a near-impossible site with a budget of almost nothing; any obvious solution would have placed the house into the hill, abutting it either to the back or front. Instead, three overlapping floors run parallel to the street and open at either end, like the levels in Lautner's Stevens House, channeling from the mountain to the open view. In their House with Five Corners (2012), an even fiercer constraint of site forced them, like

**Escher GuneWardena Architecture, model
for House with Five Corners, Los Angeles,
2012**

Lautner with the Chemosphere, to seek a shape to fit its natural and social topographics in four dimensions—vertically, in plan, as an exploration of space, and in the unfolding of motion and vista. The effects, somewhat like those of the quirky rationality of Kazuo Shinohara, find all their beauty in conforming to the logic of the situation and in its constraints.

It is evident from these examples that the current architectural culture moves marvelously in and out of tune with its precursors. It is a studio society in which there is an economy of work, where architects and their studios are scattered into storefronts and suburban homes all over the city's neighborhoods rather than squeezed into the lofts of a metropolitan design quarter, where trial and testing trump theory, new work by artists is watched as closely as that by architects, and thinking a thing and making one are the same act. Above all it is a culture governed by a certain economy of referents. There is no divorce between the preservation architect and the maker of new forms, and many practices move daily among adaptation, restoration, and an empty slate. Thus, local sources slip quietly but constantly into the best new work, appearing not as stylistic reminiscences but in the similar logic with which these younger architects treat site or situation. Similar too are their strategies for negotiating between secluded and open ground, between truth to purpose and openness to change, and between casual construction and fine design. Their designs exist in sympathy with Los Angeles' horizontal lines, the so-sharp sparseness of its shadows, and the vastness of its luminous landscapes.

Academic and Professional Timelines

These timelines are designed to convey the overlapping academic and professional galaxies of the architects featured in this catalogue. The academic timeline is organized chronologically according to the date of each firm's establishment. Names of the corresponding principals are listed, followed by the years they earned their professional degrees; the schools they attended are indicated by color bars. The professional timeline traces professional affiliations, illustrating those instances where architects working for one firm have moved on to work for others or establish their own.

UNIVERSITY OF APPLIED ARTS VIENNA

CAL POLY POMONA

CAL POLY SAN LUIS OBISPO

1990
LORCAN O'HERLIHY ARCHITECTS
Lorcan O'Herlihy, 1981
B. Arch.
M. Arch.

HARVARD

1983
FRANKLIN D. ISRAEL DESIGN ASSOCIATES
Franklin D. Israel, 1971
M. Arch.

UNIVERSITY OF FLORIDA

1990
DALY GENIK ARCHITECTS
Kevin Daly, 1985
Christopher Genik (principal from 1990–2010), 1985
M. Arch.
M. Arch.

RICE

1984
HODGETTS + FUNG
Craig Hodgetts, 1967
Hsinming Fung, 1980
M. Arch.
M. Arch.

USC

1973
COY HOWARD & COMPANY
Coy Howard, 1971
M. Arch.

1991
BROOKS + SCARPA ARCHITECTS
(formerly PUGH + SCARPA)
Lawrence Scarpa, 1997
Angela Brooks, 1991
M. Arch.
M. Arch.

1962
FRANK O. GEHRY & ASSOCIATES (became GEHRY PARTNERS in 2002)
Frank O. Gehry, 1954, 1956–57, 1984
B. Arch.
City Planning Program, Eliot Noyes Chair

1985
MARK MACK ARCHITECTS
Mark Mack, 1973
M. Arch.

1906
AC MARTIN PARTNERS

1972
MORPHOSIS ARCHITECTS
Thom Mayne, 1969, 1978
B. Arch.
M. Arch.

1992
ROTO ARCHITECTS
Michael Rotondi, 1967–69, 1969–71, 1973
B. Arch.

1969
STUDIO WORKS ARCHITECTS
Robert Mangurian, 1967
Mary-Ann Ray, 1987
B. Arch.
M. Arch.

1985
SAEE STUDIO
Michele Saee, 1981
University of Florence, M. Arch.

1973
ERIC OWEN MOSS ARCHITECTS
Eric Owen Moss, 1965, 1968, 1972
B.A.
M. Arch.
M. Arch.

1992
COSCIA DAY ARCHITECTURE AND DESIGN
Anthony Coscia, 1991
Johnathen Day, 1989
M. Arch.
B. Arch.

ACADEMY OF FINE ARTS VIENNA

1988
NEIL M. DENARI ARCHITECTS
(formerly COR-TEX ARCHITECTURE)
Neil M. Denari, 1982
M. Arch.

1995
MICHAEL MALTZAN ARCHITECTURE
Michael Maltzan, 1988
M. Arch.

UC BERKELEY

BALL STATE UNIVERSITY

COLUMBIA

1995
GREG LYNN FORM
Greg Lynn, 1988
M. Arch.

CORNELL

YALE

ARCHITECTURAL ASSOCIATION, SCHOOL OF ARCHITECTURE LONDON

1995
BESTOR
ARCHITECTURE
Barbara Bestor, 1992
M. Arch.

1996
RANDALL STOUT
ARCHITECTS
Randall Stout, 1988
M. Arch.

1997
BELZBERG
ARCHITECTS
Hagy Belzberg, 1991
M. Arch.

1998
TOURAINE RICHMOND
ARCHITECTS
Olivier Touraine
Deborah Richmond, 1994
M. Arch.

1998
JOHNSTONMARKLEE
Sharon Johnston, 1995
Mark Lee, 1991, 1995
M. Arch.
B. Arch.
M. Arch.

1999
DOISU STUDIO
ARCHITECTURE
Doris Sung, 1990
M. Arch.

1999
TOM WISCOMBE DESIGN
(formerly EMERGENT
TOM WISCOMBE)
Tom Wiscombe, 1999
M. Arch.

2000
XTEN ARCHITECTURE
Austin Kelly, 1989, 1993
Monikä Hafelfinger, 1992, 1994
B. Arch.
M. Arch.
B. Arch.
M.S.A.A.D.

2000
PREDOCK FRANE
ARCHITECTS
Hadrian Predock, 1993
John Frane, 1993
M. Arch.
B. Arch.

2000
MAKE ARCHITECTURE
William Beauter, 1997
Jess Mullen-Carey, 1993
M. Arch.
B. Arch.

2001
P-A-T-T-E-R-N-S
Marcelo Spina, 1997
Georgina Huljich, 2003
M.S.
M. Arch.

2001
B + U
Herwig Baumgartner, 1996
Scott Uriu, 1993
M. Arch.
B. Arch.

2001
PATRICK TIGHE
ARCHITECTURE
Patrick Tighe, 1993
M. Arch.

2002
BORDEN
PARTNERSHIP
Gail Peter Borden, 2000
M. Arch.

2004
ATELIER MANFERDINI
Elena Manferdini, 2000
M. Arch. / M.U.D.

2004
OYLER WU
COLLABORATIVE
Dwayne Oyler, 2001
Jenny Wu, 2001
M. Arch.
M. Arch.

2006
FPMOD
Florencia Pita, 2001
M. Arch.

2006
VOID
Arshia Mahmoodi, 1997
Shadid Beheshti University,
Tehran, M.S.A.A.D.

2007
BALL-NOGUES
STUDIO
Benjamin Ball, 1994
Gaston Nogues, 1993
B. Arch.
B. Arch.

2007
HIRSUTA
Jason Payne, 2004, 2005
B. Arch.
M.S.A.A.D

2008
MURMUR
Heather Roberge, 1995
M. Arch.

UT AUSTIN

SCI-ARC

2009
FREELANDBUCK
David Freeland, 2004
Brennan Buck, 2004
M. Arch.
M. Arch.

UNIVERSITY OF MINNESOTA

PRINCETON

2009
LAYER
Emily White, 2006
Lisa Little, 2006
M. Arch.
M. Arch.

2010
WARREN TECHENTIN
ARCHITECTURE
Warren Techentin, 1995
M. Arch./
M.A.U.D.

UCLA

OHIO STATE

GEORGIA TECH

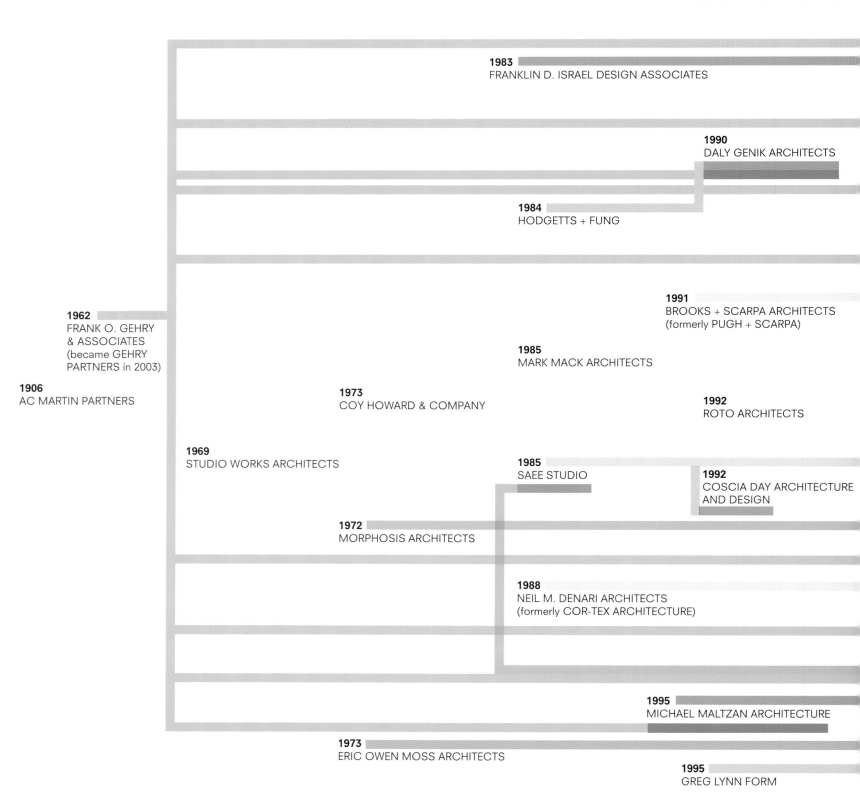

1990
LORCAN O'HERLIHY ARCHITECTS

1983
FRANKLIN D. ISRAEL DESIGN ASSOCIATES

1990
DALY GENIK ARCHITECTS

1984
HODGETTS + FUNG

1991
BROOKS + SCARPA ARCHITECTS
(formerly PUGH + SCARPA)

1962
FRANK O. GEHRY
& ASSOCIATES
(became GEHRY
PARTNERS in 2003)

1985
MARK MACK ARCHITECTS

1906
AC MARTIN PARTNERS

1973
COY HOWARD & COMPANY

1992
ROTO ARCHITECTS

1969
STUDIO WORKS ARCHITECTS

1985
SAEE STUDIO

1992
COSCIA DAY ARCHITECTURE
AND DESIGN

1972
MORPHOSIS ARCHITECTS

1988
NEIL M. DENARI ARCHITECTS
(formerly COR-TEX ARCHITECTURE)

1995
MICHAEL MALTZAN ARCHITECTURE

1973
ERIC OWEN MOSS ARCHITECTS

1995
GREG LYNN FORM

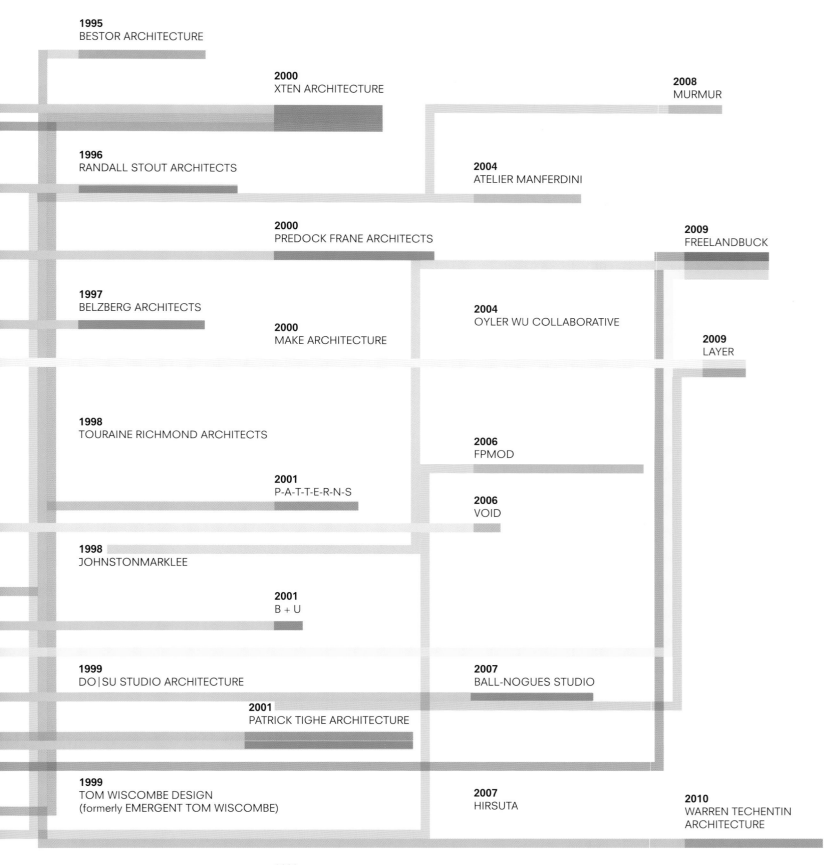

1995
BESTOR ARCHITECTURE

2000
XTEN ARCHITECTURE

2008
MURMUR

1996
RANDALL STOUT ARCHITECTS

2004
ATELIER MANFERDINI

2000
PREDOCK FRANE ARCHITECTS

2009
FREELANDBUCK

1997
BELZBERG ARCHITECTS

2004
OYLER WU COLLABORATIVE

2000
MAKE ARCHITECTURE

2009
LAYER

1998
TOURAINE RICHMOND ARCHITECTS

2006
FPMOD

2001
P-A-T-T-E-R-N-S

2006
VOID

1998
JOHNSTONMARKLEE

2001
B + U

1999
DO|SU STUDIO ARCHITECTURE

2007
BALL-NOGUES STUDIO

2001
PATRICK TIGHE ARCHITECTURE

1999
TOM WISCOMBE DESIGN
(formerly EMERGENT TOM WISCOMBE)

2007
HIRSUTA

2010
WARREN TECHENTIN
ARCHITECTURE

2002
BORDEN PARTNERSHIP

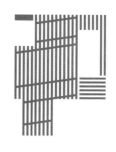

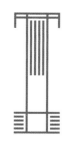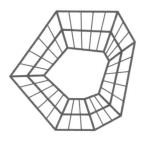

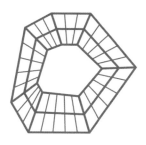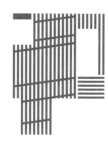

PAVILION PROPOSALS

Atelier Manferdini
Elena Manferdini

TEMPERA

The pavilion massing is a tilted cube; the simple act of tilting the cube challenges the idea of the ground in terms of gravity and stability. The outside surface is covered by 150 floral panels made of folded aluminum that are assembled onto a modular triangular structure running diagonally along the cube in loops of glossy chromatic gradients of pink and blue. The inner walls are made out of digitally printed aluminum inlays, where viewers can see their reflection inhabiting the space. Both surfaces explore novel painterly techniques able to create an immersive fantastic garden for MOCA.

The subject of the printed images challenges the principle of "still nature" through a contemporary digital use of paint and brushing techniques that constitute an expanded hybrid nature and collapses reality and artifice onto a printed canvas. The pavilion appeals to the viewer through a playful, fictional, and pop eye-candy aesthetic.

A. Interior view
B–E. Elevations
F. Unfolded
G. Physical model

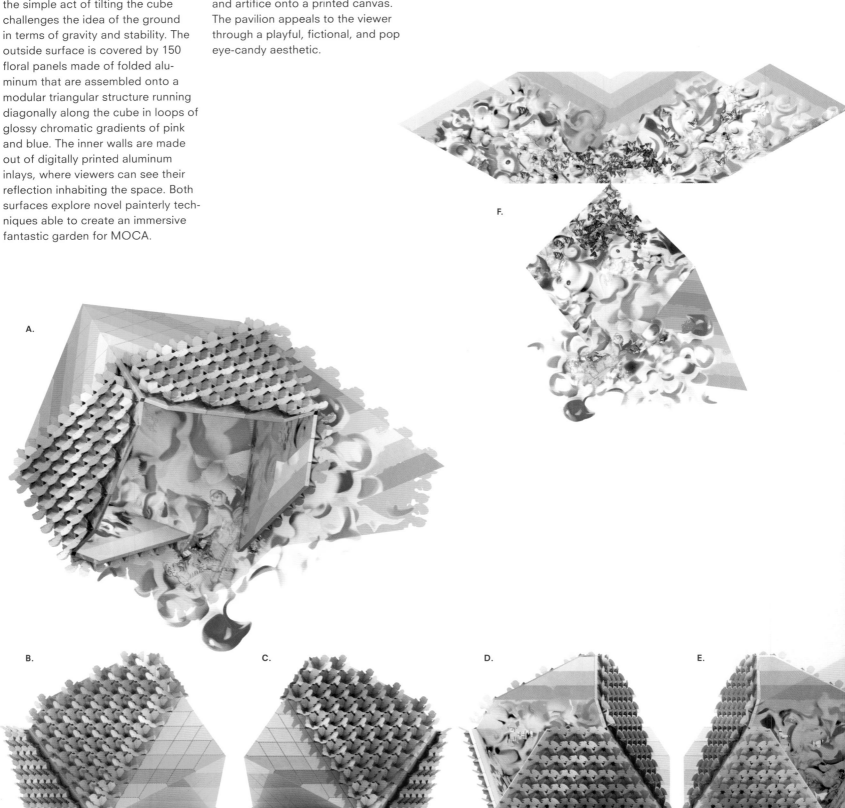

A.

F.

B.

C.

D.

E.

G.

A.

B.

C.

D.

E.

H.

G.

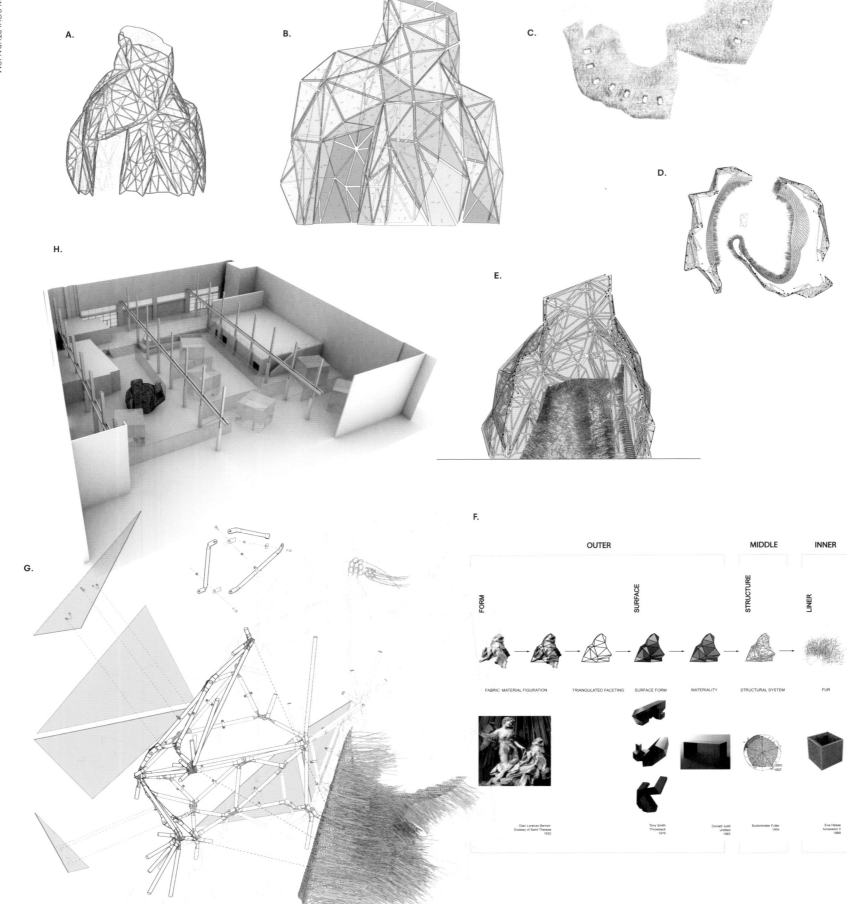

F.

OUTER | MIDDLE | INNER

FORM | SURFACE | STRUCTURE | LINER

FABRIC: MATERIAL FIGURATION | TRIANGULATED FACETING | SURFACE FORM | MATERIALITY | STRUCTURAL SYSTEM | FUR

Gian Lorenzo Bernini
Ecstasy of Saint Therese
1652

Tony Smith
Throwback
1976

Donald Judd
untitled
1965

Buckminster Fuller
1954

Eva Hesse
Accession II
1969

Borden Partnership
Gail Peter Borden

FUR-LINED

The legacy of form is derived from the material nature of its tectonics.

Fascinated by the fold, artists through the ages have spent time on its form. Michelangelo focused repeatedly on drawings of fabric. They are a way to express feeling in a building through frozen motion without using historic decoration. In this pavilion, we use the signature folds of Gian Lorenzo Bernini's flowing drapery in *The Ecstasy of St. Theresa* to inspire the form. They allow for the simulated energy of representational figuration to occur in a static form. An abstraction of material and form unite to create an erotic moment. Building on the postmodernist independence of skin from structure as a disengaged relationship that is core to Los Angeles architecture, the pavilion accelerates the condition. Three layers, each with its own material and manufacturing technology, engage and push the Gehry methodology of a differentiated skin and structural system. Independently defined and formed components, tasked with varied experiences, the dialogue between the elements generates a new and dynamic conversation. Synthesizing the intention of the fold with the geometry and materiality of Pop art, Minimalism, and geometric abstraction originating in Southern California in the 1960s, the pavilion emerges from the tectonics of place aligned through the lineage of architectural thought. Refocused on light and space, the form and material become dynamic players in their conversation.

I.

J.

K.

A. System structure
B. System Plexi-panels
C. System fur
D. Plan
E. Section
F. Morphology diagrams
G. 3-layers detail
H. Site rendering
I–K. Views of case and contents
L. Rendering of exterior

L.

DO|SU Studio Architecture
Doris Sung

BLINK

Blink resourcefully and comprehensively embodies the three Vitruvian virtues of architecture: *utilitas*, *firmitas*, and *venustas*.

1. *Utilitas*: The proposed pavilion is designed to manually roll to vary the amount of public or private space within. The utility of this dynamic enclosure is immediately evident when various social encounters and joint effort are required to move the large, lightweight structure. Like its name, it "blinks" open and closed.

2. *Firmitas*: Firmness, on the other hand, is expressed in its innovative self-structuring tectonics that takes full form and strength when cooled to room temperature. Using high temperatures as a construction technique is unusual in architecture, but necessary when working with new shape-memory alloys. It allows the contractor to use one hand in assembly and simple tools.

3. *Venustas*: Primarily made of smart thermobimetal, which automatically curls when heated, the pavilion embodies the virtue of delight in its unusual saddle shape and natural surface finish. By use of the digital medium and fabrication, the shape and form can be complex and fluid.

D.

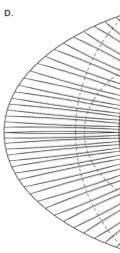

C.

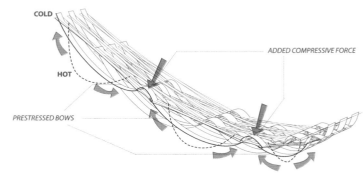

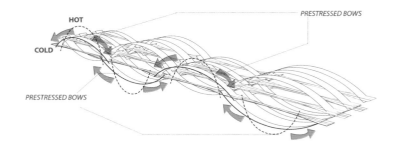

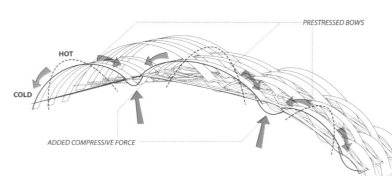

A.

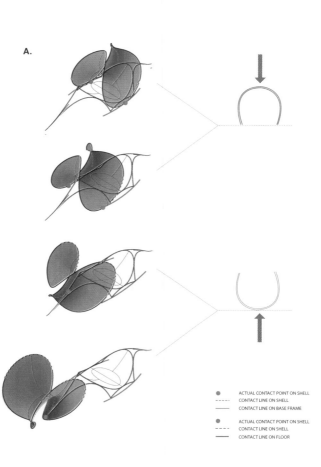

ACTUAL CONTACT POINT ON SHELL
CONTACT LINE ON SHELL
CONTACT LINE ON BASE FRAME
ACTUAL CONTACT POINT ON SHELL
CONTACT LINE ON SHELL
CONTACT LINE ON FLOOR

B.

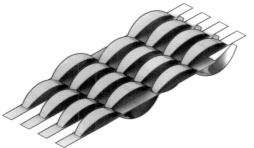

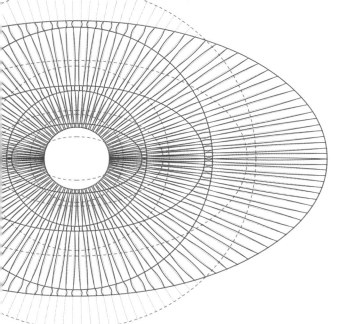

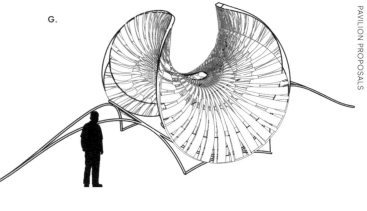

A. Structural support diagram
B. Construction sequence diagram
C. Structural surface diagram
D. Surface pattern diagram
E. Renderings
F. Perspective diagram
G. Construction sequence diagram

G.

F.

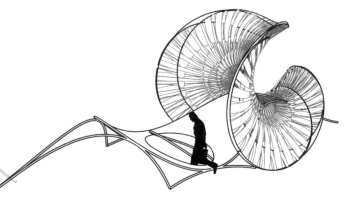

E.

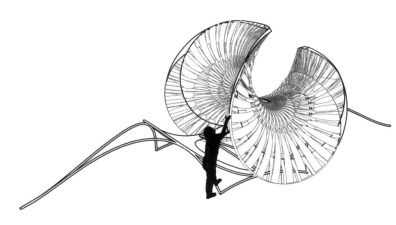

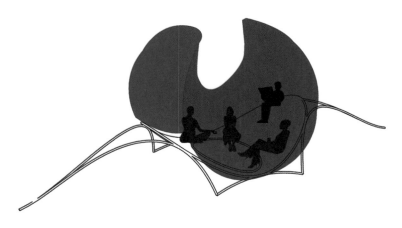

FPMOD
Florencia Pita

SITTING PRETTY

The function of this folly is that of a sitting room, where people sit (indeed), and lounge, and chat, and even (maybe) sleep. It is "composed" of three over-scaled chair-columns. The lower profiles of each one of the chair-columns makes direct reference to the elevation contour of paradigmatic chairs, from Le Corbusier's Chaise Lounge to Verner Panton's Living Tower and Frank Gehry's Easy Edges Bar Stool. The folly, *Sitting Pretty*, takes the original profiles and extrudes them, expanding the width, allowing more guests to share a place to sit (8 chairs=15 people). The upper volumes present a semi-enclosed canopy to the seating area below, acting as a gazebo. Highly ornamented objects bound the sitting area that is clad with bright shingles and set in contrast to the open landscape of the museum space beyond.

A.

B.

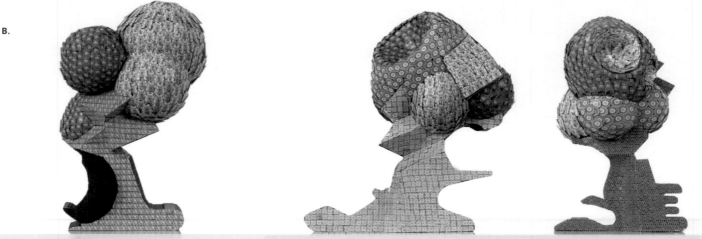

The function of this Folly is that of a Sitting Room, where people sit (indeed), and lounge, and chat, and even (maybe) sleep. It is 'composed' of three over scaled chair-columns. The lower PROFILES of each one of the chair-columns makes direct references to the elevation contour of paradigmatic chairs, from Le Corbusier's 'Chaise Lounge' to Verner Panton's 'Living Tower' and Frank Gehry's 'Easy Edges Bar Stool'. The Folly, SITTING PRETTY, takes the original profiles and extrudes them expanding the width, allowing more guests to share a place to sit (8 chairs=15 people). The upper volumes present a semi-enclosed canopy to the seating area below, acting as a 'Gazebo'. Highly ornamented objects bound the sitting area that is clad with bright shingles and set in contrast to the open landscape of the museum space beyond.

C.

Ball Chair
Designer . Eero Aarnio
Year . 1963

Thonet Rocking Chair
Designer . Michael Thonet
Year . 1860

Le Corbusier Chaise Lounge
Designer . Le Corbusier
Year . 1928

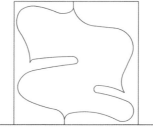

Living Tower
Designer . Verner Panton
Year . 1969

Easy Edges Bar Stool
Designer . Frank Gehry
Year . 1969

A–B. Views of model components
C. Elevation contours of paradigmatic chairs
D. Floor plan
E. Photomontage

D.

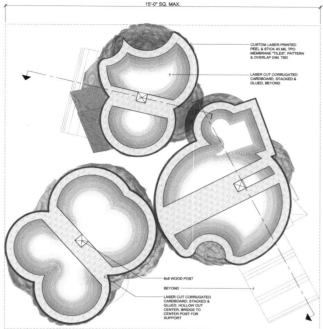

15'-0" SQ. MAX.

CUSTOM LASER-PRINTED
PEEL & STICK 45 MIL TPO
MEMBRANE "TILES", PATTERN
& OVERLAP DIM. TBD

LASER CUT CORRUGATED
CARDBOARD, STACKED &
GLUED, BEYOND

6x6 WOOD POST
BEYOND

LASER CUT CORRUGATED
CARDBOARD, STACKED &
GLUED, HOLLOW OUT
CENTER, BRIDGE TO
CENTER POST FOR
SUPPORT

E.

1. Fabrication

2. Assemble Facets

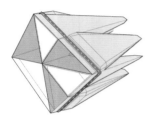

3. Aggregate Groups

A.

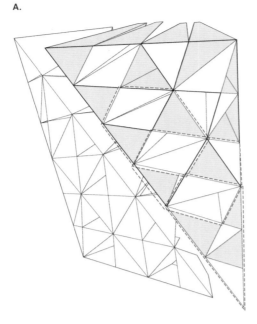

4. Tilt-Up Installation

B.

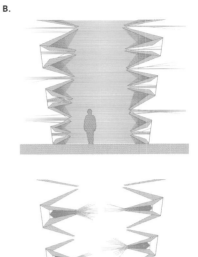

A. Lightweight assembly of foam
cones held together in tension with
fabric straps
B. Internal soundscape (top) and
speaker placement (bottom) create
variable local sound fields
C. Plan showing light and sound
filtered through the stacked cones
D. Section showing the planar exterior
surfaces, which conceal a cocoonlike
formal intricacy on the interior
E–F. Rendering of pattern/massing
G. The proposal consists of stacked
"solid" and "void" cones

G.

FreelandBuck
David Freeland and Brennan Buck

LISTENING PAVILION

Alternately massive and porous, translucent and opaque, this proposal for a listening room creates affective visual and aural fields within and around the pavilion. The aggregated nature of the pavilion's mass reflects an architectural interest in digitally orchestrated assemblies of parts. At the same time, the solid/void stack, together with layered finishes and acoustic coatings, create an ambiguous materiality reminiscent of the art of the California Light and Space movement. The cocoonlike formal intricacy of the interior is reminiscent of anechoic chambers, absorbing ambient sound to create a multisensory respite from the museum.

C.

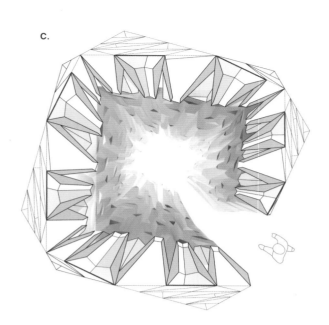

D.

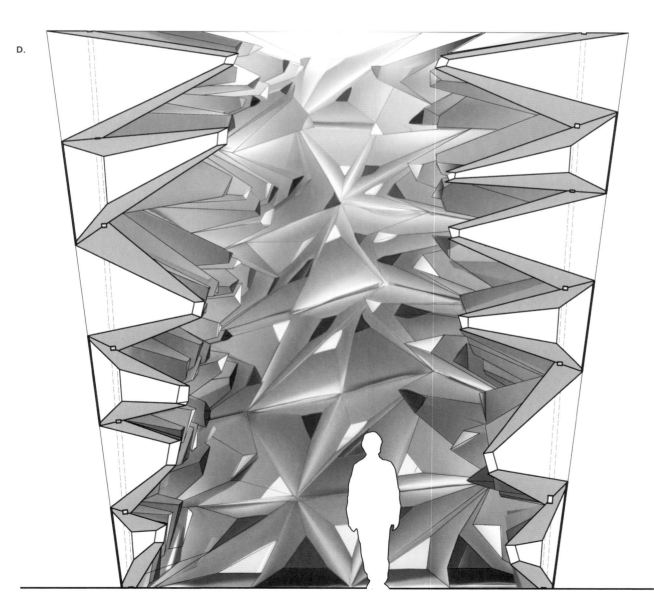

E.

F.

Hirsuta
Jason Payne

MATHILDE: LOW ALBEDO

Asteroids are profoundly closed
objects, their observation possible
only from without and from afar. In
this way their relation to us is one of
constant recession, a turning away,
a deep ambivalence to our ever
knowing them. But what if one were
to let us in, to let us see it from the
inside? This project imagines asteroid
253 Mathilde turned outside-in,
making space of the object. An
impulse to construct a very strange
and dark form, *Mathilde: Low
Albedo* initiates a new foray into
the old problem of the subject-
object relationship. In the context
of MOCA's "A New Sculpturalism"
exhibition this seems wholly reasonable; after all, the impulse to create
unorthodox form surely must be the
deepest link that ties the otherwise
heterogeneous cohort that is this
show's cast of characters.

F.

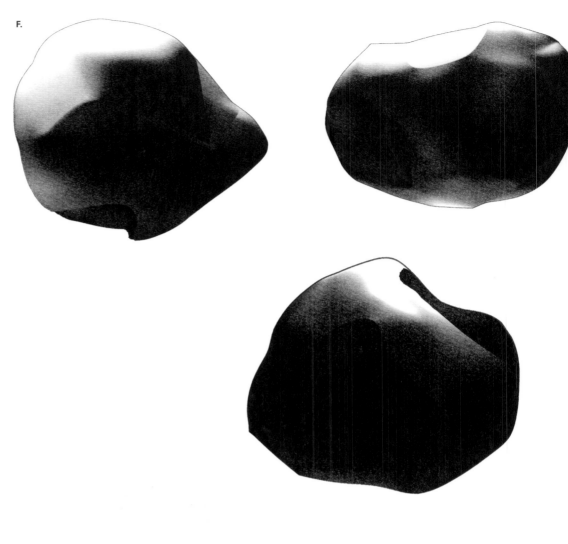

A.

B.

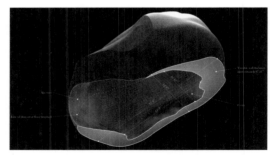

C.

A. Typical igloo construction from Norbert E. Yankielun, *How to Build an Igloo and Other Snow Shelters*, 2007, illustration by Amelia Bauer
B. Worm's-eye view
C. Typical igloo in construction by Innuit Tookillkee Kiguktak of Griese Fiord, Ellesmere Island, from Ulli Steltzer, *Building an Igloo*, 1981
D. Elevation showing creases in its geometry, their visibility augmented here through wireframe overlay, which corresponds to edges of foam blocks stacked in the fashion of igloo construction
E. Section
F. Rendered views of Mathilde in rotation

E.

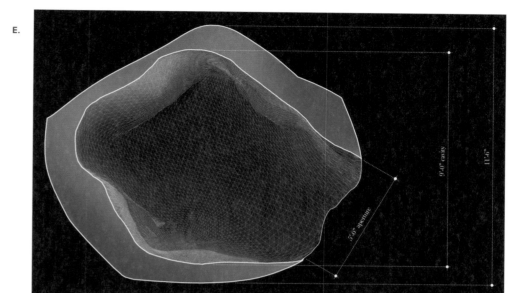

D.

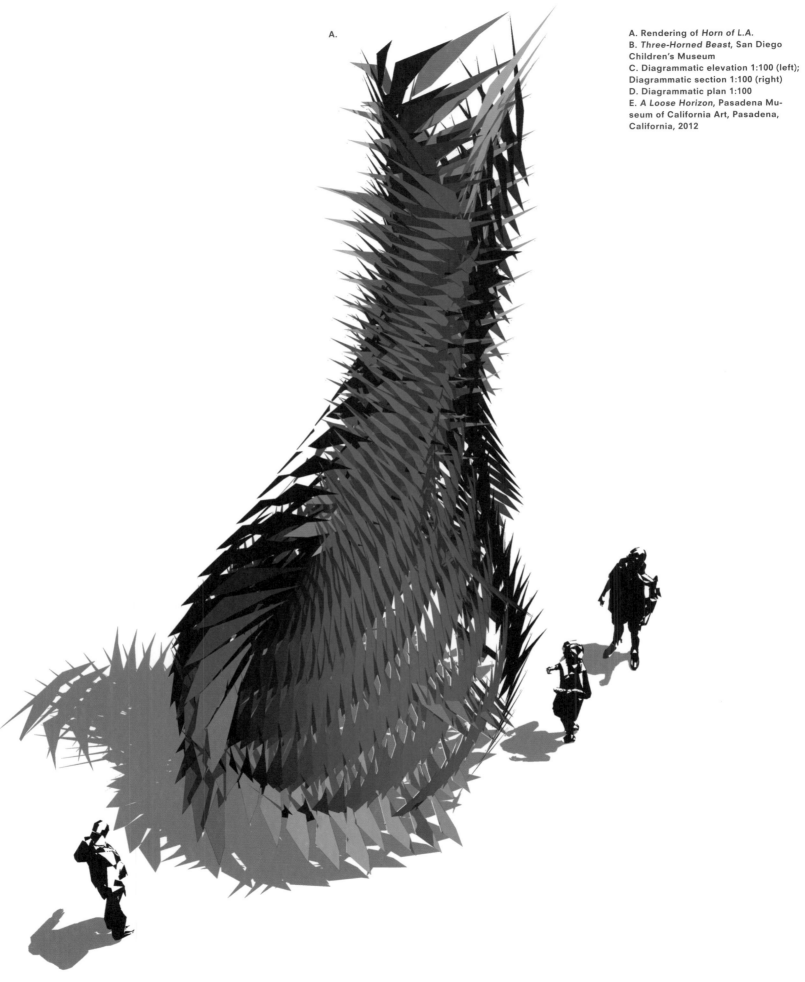

A.

A. Rendering of *Horn of L.A.*
B. *Three-Horned Beast*, San Diego
Children's Museum
C. Diagrammatic elevation 1:100 (left);
Diagrammatic section 1:100 (right)
D. Diagrammatic plan 1:100
E. *A Loose Horizon*, Pasadena Museum of California Art, Pasadena,
California, 2012

Layer
Emily White and Lisa Little

HORN OF L.A.

The *Horn of L.A.* is for lounging and listening. Its exterior is a scaly shell and its interior has stuffed seating where visitors can sit and listen to an audio component of the exhibition.

The Horn belongs to a trajectory of folded aluminum structures Layer has been developing through a series of similarly scaled projects. In this instance the pavilion's shell is composed of two interleaved shapes, one basketlike, the other frondlike. Its texture ranges from smooth and laminar near the floor level seating to more erratic at the top. A particular interest in this pavilion is the potential of interleaving to create rigidity in the shell while allowing a bit of rustle in the uppermost fronds.

B.

C.

D.

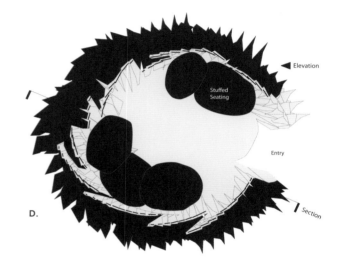

E.

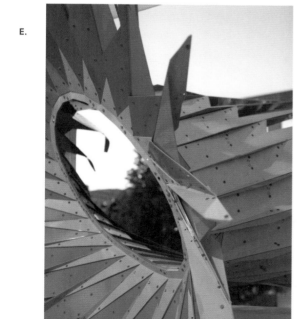  

Murmur
Heather Roberge

ULTRAVIOLET

Ultraviolet collapses numerous trajectories of architectural and cultural production into a surprisingly thin shell. Its five-millimeter-thick aluminum shell is thermoformed and robotically trimmed using aerospace manufacturing techniques. The project's self-supporting skin foregrounds spatial effects and material expression by eliminating a separate structural frame. A vibrant coating of violet flocking fibers, found in elements of product and fashion design, envelopes the interior spaces, creating intimate areas for resting. Rigid in construction but supple in its spatial effects, *Ultraviolet* evokes associations with objects from high and popular culture such as Richard Serra's *Torqued Ellipse* series and Alvar Aalto's glass vases and vinyl figurines as a means to heighten audience engagement. Under the influence of these cultural and technological forces, Ultraviolet swerves the tectonic and spatial possibilities of architecture.

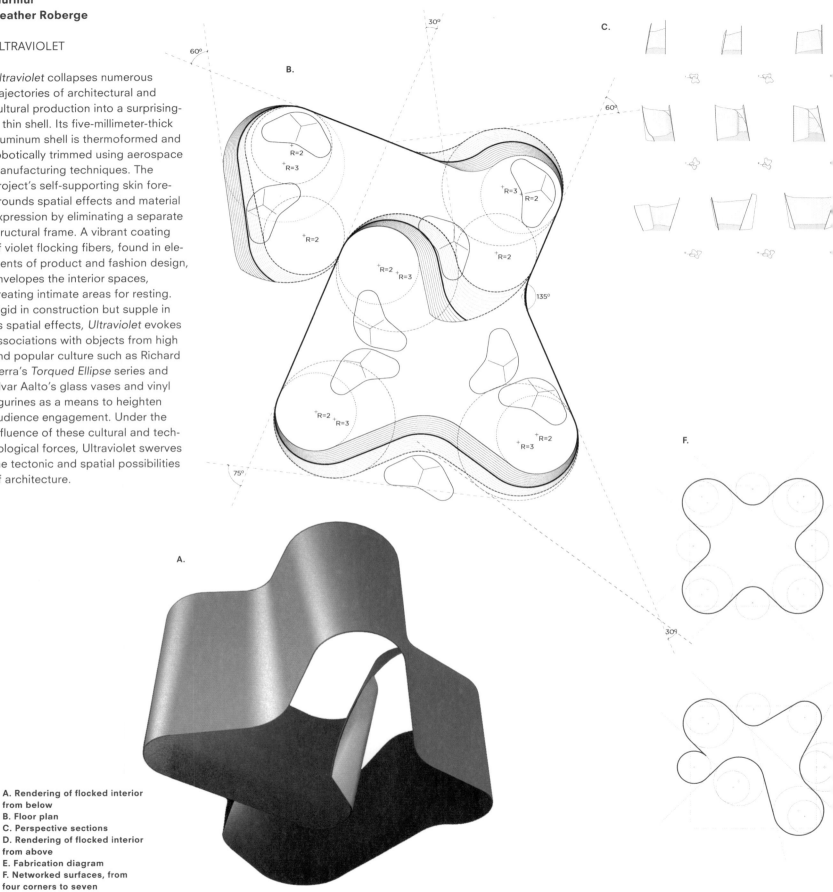

A. Rendering of flocked interior from below
B. Floor plan
C. Perspective sections
D. Rendering of flocked interior from above
E. Fabrication diagram
F. Networked surfaces, from four corners to seven

D.

E.

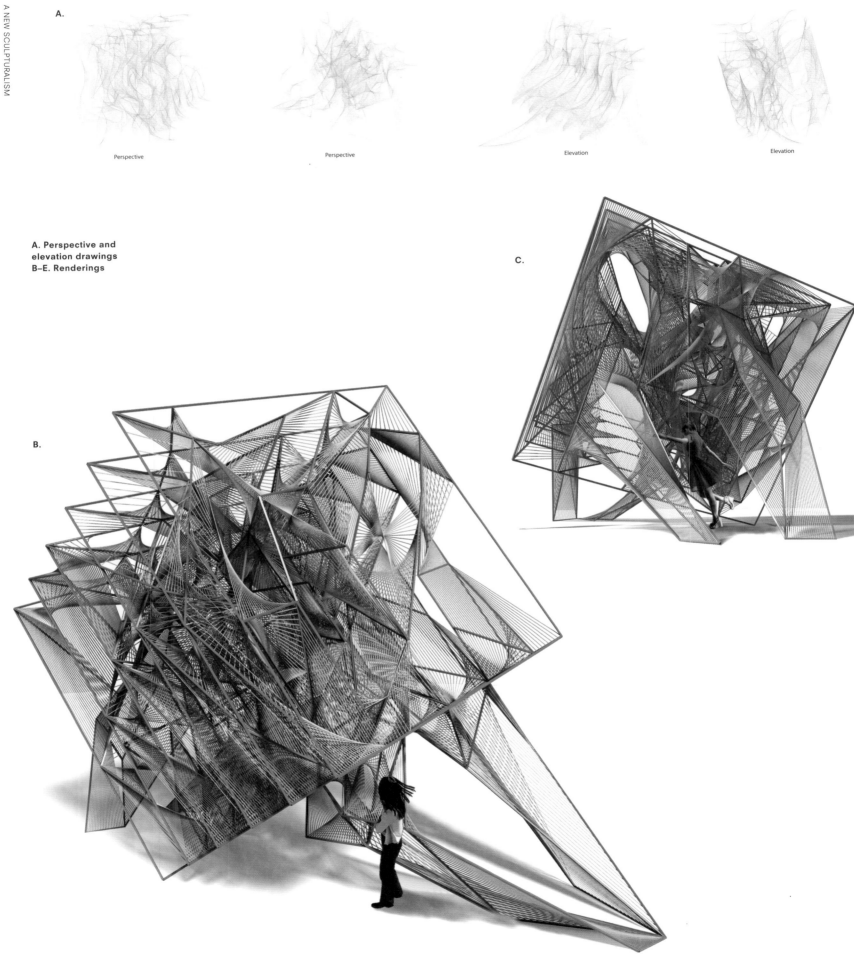

A.

Perspective

Perspective

Elevation

Elevation

A. Perspective and
elevation drawings
B–E. Renderings

C.

B.

Oyler Wu Collaborative
Dwayne Oyler and Jenny Wu

THE DRAWING ROOM

Our pavilion proposal (and, in fact, our primary interest as architects) has been shaped by two key obsessions that have been constant in the work of Southern California architects over the last twenty-five years. The first is in the relentlessly exploratory nature of representational line-work. Often employed as much more than a conventional "representation" tool, line has become an abstract language in and of itself, often demanding creative interpretations and nuanced readings in order to arrive at a tangible outcome. Line, for example, simultaneously describes trajectory and edge of plane, as well as "latent" descriptive geometries. The second interest has been the persistent desire to give coherent spatial characteristics to these two-dimensional representations. The process essentially imagines possibilities for how the line-work might be occupied through some architectural translation.

Our proposal is aimed at merging these interests into a complex, three-dimensional spatial experience, one that capitalizes directly on the inherent spatial characteristics of line. By using a semi-repetitious field of twisting "surfaces," the proposal oscillates between complex field and coherent geometric pattern. Ultimately, we are interested in the transcendence of line into a completely engulfing experience—one that can be occupied as a kind of three-dimensional drawing. This ambition is aimed at raising the level of curiosity about the nature of line-work, from geometric object, to a sense of enclosure, to a dynamic field of shifting trajectories.

The design process began with a simple two-dimensional plane with a series of patterns, consisting of line-work, drawn across the surface. That surface is then repeated in space, creating six planes, each offset a distance of thirty-six inches from one another, forming a perfect cube. As the planes within that cube are offset, each transforms, requiring the planes of lines to adapt, twist, and contort in order to maintain a connective relationship with the next. This creates cavities of space formed by continuously warping planes that reach deep into the volume. Eventually, the planes spill out of the volume, lifting the volume into the air, becoming structural supports for the now precariously tilted volume of lines.

E.

D.

P-A-T-T-E-R-N-S
Marcelo Spina and Georgina Huljich, in collaboration with Bill Pearson of North Sails

THE TEXTILE ROOM

The Textile Room aims to physically stage a direct response to the exhibition brief set up by the curator, following the tradition of formal experimentation and material innovation in Southern California that the show embodies. *The Textile Room* illuminates the possibilities of extreme lightweight materials in architecture, by producing a supple, quasi-rigid, and clothlike space that physically and experientially blurs the threshold between hard and soft, textile and tectonic, intimate and public. The radiating patterns are constructed of aramid and carbon fiber tape developed in collaboration with North Sails Composites division, producing varying densities and a vast range of opacities.

A. Floor plan
B. Diagrams
C. Unfolded plan
D. Interior perspective

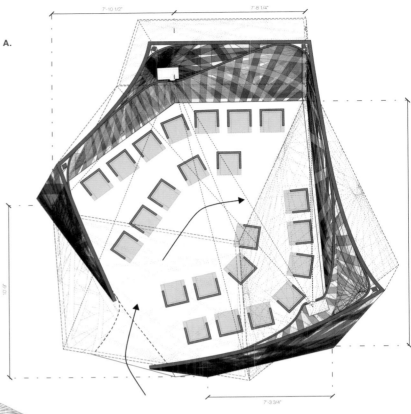
A.

C.

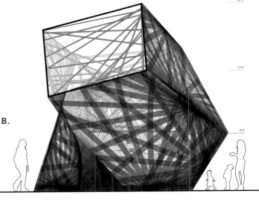
B.

D.

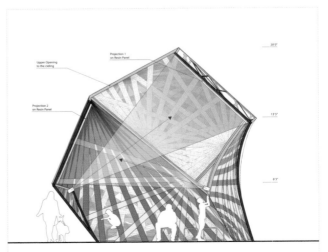

Predock_Frane Architects
Hadrian Predock and John Frane

LIGHT SPACE

Our proposal for the MOCA pavilion extends from the idea that the implicit star of "A New Sculpturalism" is the City of Los Angeles itself. Posited as a "love letter" to the city from architecture, our design is a voluptuous sculptural object on the outside and an enveloping cyclorama of the city grids on the inside. Placed within the geographic center of an exhibition field of dynamic visuals and shifting media, we propose a pavilion that allows for a pause from the exhibition, reorienting the visitor to their position in space relative to the cardinal directions and the city grids. This is a resting space that prompts a new registration of the exhibited architectural projects by understanding a greater context that unites the work.

A. Rendering in 2-D line drawing
B. Interior view
C. Axo shape
D. Scheme of pavilion in four pieces
E. Study renderings

A.

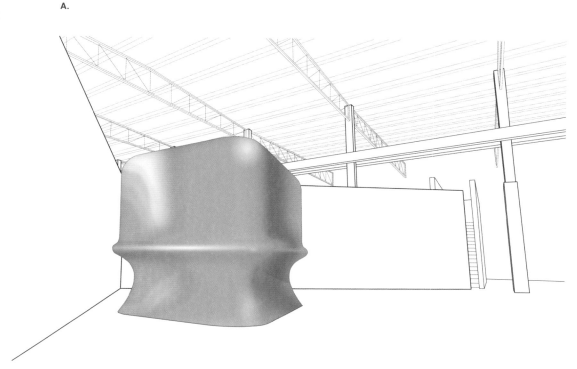

E.

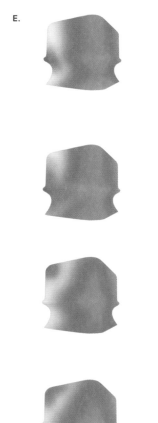

B.

D.

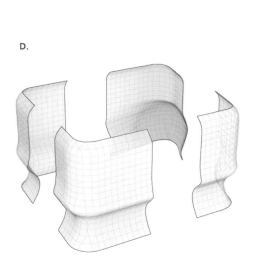

C.

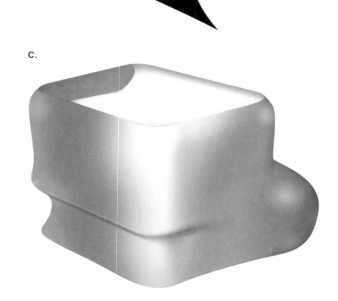

A. Rendering in 2-D line drawing
B. Interior view
C. Axo shape
D. Scheme of pavilion in four pieces
E. Study renderings

Tom Wiscombe Design
Tom Wiscombe

MASS PAINTING II

This pavilion is a study of surface-to-volume transformations, where mass is achieved by pushing into a surface like a fist through a rubber sheet. In this case, chunky figures are pushed into the exterior skin of the pavilion, creating volumetric effects on the interior. The perimeter edge of the large aperture in the piece is razor-thin, creating visual tension between the realms of 2-D/flat and 3-D/spatial extension.

In order to de-couple exterior character from interior character, the surface delaminates. The outer surface becomes hard and defines a crystalline profile and silhouette of the object in space, while the inner surface becomes soft, defining a supple interior world. The two surfaces maintain a loose relationship, sometimes fusing together, other times producing thick poche zones that cannot be directly seen or measured by the observer.

A pattern of computational tattoos emphasizes the transformation from surface to volume while also maximizing the atmospheric difference between interior and exterior. These tattoos break down the inner surface into a multi-material manifold, where glossy white plastic switches to metallic green foil and then to black textured felt. These synthetic material effects will be fake and applied as surface treatment to a molded composite substrate.

The project is projected to be built in part using local entertainment industry resources such as Warner Studios for thermoforming and/or CNC milling and Disney for painting. Alley 36, a design build company in Los Angeles, will coordinate the effort and deliver the project.

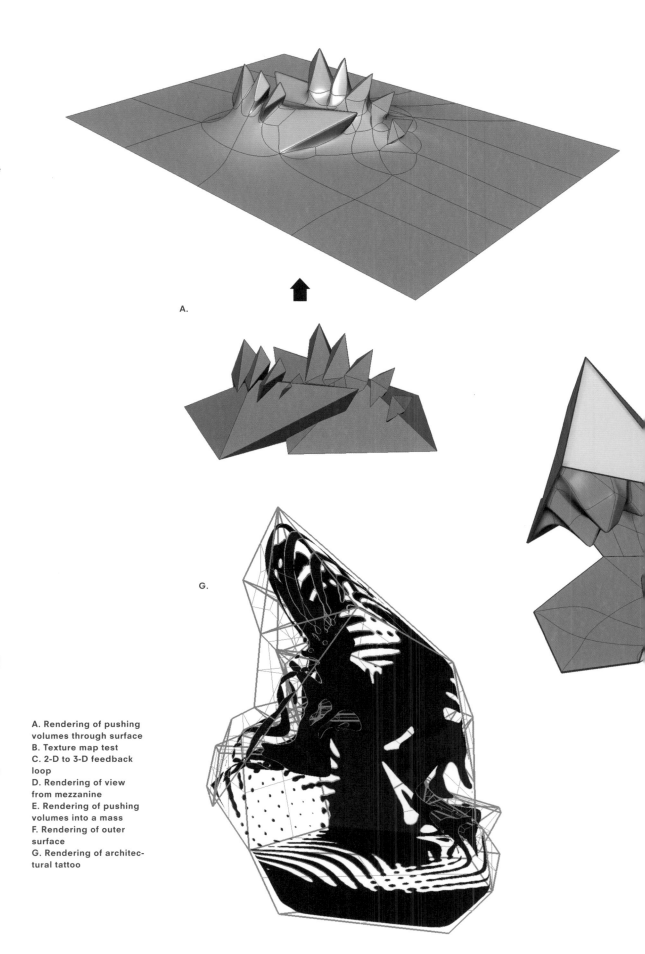

A.

G.

A. Rendering of pushing volumes through surface
B. Texture map test
C. 2-D to 3-D feedback loop
D. Rendering of view from mezzanine
E. Rendering of pushing volumes into a mass
F. Rendering of outer surface
G. Rendering of architectural tattoo

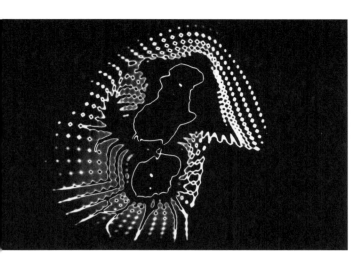

B.

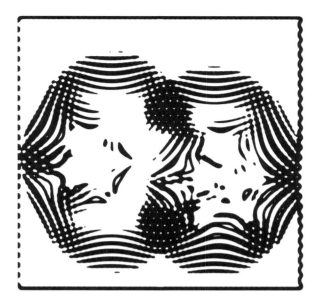

C.

F.

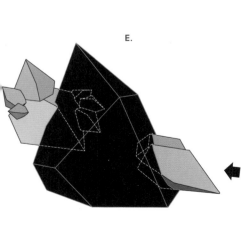

E.

D.

Selected Projects
Relevant to the Exhibition

AC MARTIN PARTNERS

P208–9
Hollenbeck Replacement Police Station, 2009

Location: Los Angeles
Clients: Los Angeles Police Department, Hollenbeck Community Police Station, and the City of Los Angeles, Bureau of Engineering
Architect: AC Martin Partners
Principals: Christopher C. Martin, FAIA; Ken Lewis, AIA; David C. Martin, FAIA; and Carey McLeod, AIA

BALL-NOGUES STUDIO

P7, P210
Maximilian's Schell, **2005**

Location: Los Angeles
Client: Materials & Applications
Architect: Ball-Nogues Studio
Principals: Benjamin Ball and Gaston Nogues

P213
Liquid Sky, **2007**

Location: Long Island City, New York
Client: MoMA PS1
Architect: Ball-Nogues Studio
Principals: Benjamin Ball and Gaston Nogues

P211
Feathered Edge, **2009**

Location: Los Angeles
Client: Museum of Contemporary Art, Los Angeles
Architect: Ball-Nogues Studio
Principals: Benjamin Ball and Gaston Nogues

P212
Table Cloth for the Courtyard at Schoenberg Hall, **2010**

Location: Herb Alpert School of Music, University of California, Los Angeles
Client: University of California, Los Angeles
Architect: Ball-Nogues Studio
Principals: Benjamin Ball and Gaston Nogues

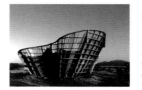

P214–15
Yucca Crater, **2011**

Location: Near Twentynine Palms, California
Client: High Desert Test Sites
Architect: Ball-Nogues Studio
Principals: Benjamin Ball and Gaston Nogues

BELZBERG ARCHITECTS

P17
Skyline Residence, 2007

Location: Los Angeles
Client: Skyline, LLC
Architect: Belzberg Architects
Principal: Hagy Belzberg, FAIA

P10, P162–63
Los Angeles Museum of the Holocaust, 2010

Location: Los Angeles
Clients: Los Angeles Museum of the Holocaust (Building) / City of Los Angeles (Land)
Architect: Belzberg Architects
Principal: Hagy Belzberg, FAIA

P164
9800 Wilshire Boulevard, 2012

Location: Beverly Hills, California
Client: Alec Gores, The Gores Group
Architect: Belzberg Architects
Principal: Hagy Belzberg, FAIA

BESTOR ARCHITECTURE

P5, P134
Floating Bungalow, 2009

Location: Los Angeles
Client: Eric Grunbaum
Architect: Bestor Architecture
Principal: Barbara Bestor, AIA

BROOKS + SCARPA ARCHITECTS

P186–87
Bergamot Artist Lofts, 1999

Location: Santa Monica, California
Clients: Bergamot Station, LLC, and City of Santa Monica
Architect: Brooks + Scarpa Architects (formerly Pugh + Scarpa)
Principals: Angela Brooks, AIA, and Lawrence Scarpa, FAIA

P188
Orange Grove, 2004

Location: West Hollywood, California
Client: Urban Environments, Inc.
Architect: Brooks + Scarpa Architects (formerly Pugh + Scarpa)
Principals: Angela Brooks, AIA, and Lawrence Scarpa, FAIA

P188–89
Cherokee Mixed-Use Lofts, 2010

Location: Los Angeles
Client: REthink Development, Inc.
Architect: Brooks + Scarpa Architects (formerly Pugh + Scarpa)
Principals: Angela Brooks, AIA, and Lawrence Scarpa, FAIA

B + U

P12, P206–7
Frank and Kim Residence, 2010

Location: Pasadena, California
Clients: John Frank and Diann Kim
Architect: B + U
Principals: Herwig Baumgartner, AIA, and Scott Uriu, AIA

COSCIA DAY ARCHITECTURE AND DESIGN

P168
Natalee Thai, 2000

Location: Culver City, California
Client: Victor Watana
Architect: Coscia Day Architecture and Design
Principals: Anthony Coscia and Johnathen Day

P168–69
Skywave House, 2010

Location: Los Angeles
Client: Anthony Coscia
Architect: Coscia Day Architecture and Design
Principals: Anthony Coscia and Johnathen Day

COY HOWARD & COMPANY

P113
Ellen and Jay McCafferty House, 1980

Location: San Pedro, California
Clients: Ellen and Jay McCafferty
Architect: Coy Howard & Company
Principal: Coy Howard

P112
Ashley House, 1989

Location: Chino, California
Clients: Lee and Joe Ashley
Architect: Coy Howard & Company
Principal: Coy Howard

DALY GENIK ARCHITECTS

P136
Camino Nuevo Charter Academy, 2000

Location: Los Angeles
Client: Pueblo Nuevo Development
Architect: Daly Genik Architects
Principals: Kevin Daly, FAIA, principal-in-charge, and Christopher Genik, AIA, consulting principal

P13, P137
Art Center College of Design South Campus, 2004

Location: Pasadena, California
Client: Art Center College of Design
Architect: Daly Genik Architects
Principal: Kevin Daly, FAIA

P18–19, P138
Camino Nuevo High School, 2006

Location: Los Angeles
Client: Pueblo Nuevo Development
Architect: Daly Genik Architects
Principal: Kevin Daly, FAIA

P26, P139
Winnett, 2007

Location: Santa Monica, California
Clients: Allen Yamashita and Salvatore Satullo
Architect: Daly Genik Architects
Principal: Kevin Daly, FAIA

P140
Tahiti Affordable Housing, 2009

Location: Santa Monica, California
Client: Community Corporation of Santa Monica
Architect: Daly Genik Architects
Principal: Kevin Daly, FAIA

P14, P141
Palms House, 2011

Location: Los Angeles
Clients: Sam Laybourne and Herran Bekele
Architect: Daly Genik Architects
Principal: Kevin Daly, FAIA

ERIC OWEN MOSS ARCHITECTS

P100–1
Lawson-Westen House, 1993

Location: Los Angeles
Clients: Linda Lawson and Tracy Westen
Architect: Eric Owen Moss Architects
Principal: Eric Owen Moss, FAIA

P104
The Box, 1994

Location: Culver City, California
Client: Samitaur Constructs, Frederick and Laurie Samitaur Smith
Architect: Eric Owen Moss Architects
Principal: Eric Owen Moss, FAIA

P102–3
Samitaur, 1996

Location: Culver City, California
Client: Samitaur Constructs, Frederick and Laurie Samitaur Smith
Architect: Eric Owen Moss Architects
Principal: Eric Owen Moss, FAIA

P106–7
3535 Hayden, 1997

Location: Los Angeles
Client: Samitaur Constructs, Frederick and Laurie Samitaur Smith
Architect: Eric Owen Moss Architects
Principal: Eric Owen Moss, FAIA

P109
Umbrella, 1999

Location: Culver City, California
Client: Samitaur Constructs, Frederick and Laurie Samitaur Smith
Architect: Eric Owen Moss Architects
Principal: Eric Owen Moss, FAIA

P107
Beehive, 2001

Location: Culver City, California
Client: Samitaur Constructs, Frederick and Laurie Samitaur Smith
Architect: Eric Owen Moss Architects
Principal: Eric Owen Moss, FAIA

P104–5
Stealth, 2001

Location: Culver City, California
Client: Samitaur Constructs, Frederick and Laurie Samitaur Smith
Architect: Eric Owen Moss Architects
Principal: Eric Owen Moss, FAIA

P11
Samitaur Tower, 2010

Location: Culver City, California
Client: Samitaur Constructs, Frederick and Laurie Samitaur Smith
Architect: Eric Owen Moss Architects
Principal: Eric Owen Moss, FAIA

P109
Pterodactyl, 2013

Location: Culver City, California
Client: Samitaur Constructs, Frederick and Laurie Samitaur Smith
Architect: Eric Owen Moss Architects
Principal: Eric Owen Moss, FAIA

P108
Jefferson Tower, 2014 (projected completion)

Location: Los Angeles
Client: Samitaur Constructs, Frederick and Laurie Samitaur Smith
Architect: Eric Owen Moss Architects
Principal: Eric Owen Moss, FAIA

FRANKLIN D. ISRAEL DESIGN ASSOCIATES

P65
Lamy-Newton Pavilion, 1988

Location: Los Angeles
Client: Michele Lamy and Richard Newton
Architect: Franklin D. Israel Design Associates
Principal: Franklin D. Israel

P60, P63
Arango-Berry House, 1989

Location: Beverly Hills, California
Client: Marisa Arango and Bill Berry
Architect: Franklin D. Israel Design Associates
Principal: Franklin D. Israel

P61
Goldberg-Bean House, 1991

Location: Los Angeles
Client: Howard Goldberg and Jim Bean
Architect: Franklin D. Israel Design Associates
Principal: Franklin D. Israel

P62, P88
Drager House, 1994

Location: Berkeley, California
Client: Sharon Drager
Architect: Franklin D. Israel Design Associates
Principal: Franklin D. Israel

P64
Dan House, 1995

Location: Malibu, California
Client: Michael and Cecilia Dan
Architect: Israel, Callas, Shortridge Design Associates
Principals: Franklin D. Israel; Barbara Callas, AIA; and Steven Shortridge, AIA

P41, P65
Fine Arts Building, University of California, Riverside, 2001

Location: Riverside, California
Client: University of California, Riverside
Architect: Israel, Callas, Shortridge Design Associates
Principals: Franklin D. Israel, Barbara Callas, AIA, and Steven Shortridge, AIA
Project Designer: Annie Chu, AIA

FRANK O. GEHRY & ASSOCIATES / GEHRY PARTNERS

P48
Vitra Design Museum, 1989

Location: Weil am Rhein, Germany
Client: Vitra International, Ltd.
Architect: Frank O. Gehry & Associates
Principal: Frank O. Gehry, FAIA

P46–47
Frederick R. Weisman Art and Teaching Museum, 1993

Location: Minneapolis
Client: University of Minnesota
Architect: Frank O. Gehry & Associates
Principal: Frank O. Gehry, FAIA

P46
Team Disneyland Administration Building, 1995

Location: Anaheim, California
Client: Disney Development Company
Architect: Frank O. Gehry & Associates
Principal: Frank O. Gehry, FAIA

P49
Nationale-Nederlanden Building, 1996

Location: Prague
Client: Nationale-Nederlanden/ International Netherlands Group, represented by Yan Scheere and Paul Koch
Architect: Frank O. Gehry & Associates
Principal: Frank O. Gehry, FAIA
Collaborating Architect: Studio V. H.

P45
Guggenheim Museum, 1997

Location: Bilbao, Spain
Clients: Consorcio del Proyecto Guggenheim (Basque Country Administration) and Solomon R. Guggenheim Foundation
Architect: Frank O. Gehry & Associates
Principal: Frank O. Gehry, FAIA

P50–51
Der Neue Zollhof, 1999

Location: Düsseldorf
Client: Kunst- und Medienzentrum Rheinhafen GmbH
Architect: Frank O. Gehry & Associates
Principal: Frank O. Gehry, FAIA

P51
Experience Music Project, 2000

Location: Seattle
Client: Experience Music Project, represented by Paul G. Allen
Architect: Frank O. Gehry & Associates
Principal: Frank O. Gehry, FAIA

P2–3, P84
Walt Disney Concert Hall, 2003

Location: Los Angeles
Client: Music Center of L.A. County
Architect: Gehry Partners
Principal: Frank O. Gehry, FAIA

P52–53
Ray and Maria Stata Center, Massachusetts Institute of Technology, 2004

Location: Cambridge, Massachusetts
Client: Massachusetts Institute of Technology
Architect: Gehry Partners
Principal: Frank O. Gehry, FAIA

P54
MARTa Museum, 2005

Location: Herford, Germany
Client: The City of Herford, Germany
Architect: Gehry Partners
Principal: Frank O. Gehry, FAIA

P54–55
Hotel Marqués de Riscal, 2006

Location: Elciego, Spain
Client: Vinos Herederos del Marqués de Riscal
Architect: Gehry Partners
Principal: Frank O. Gehry, FAIA

P56
Novartis Campus, 2009

Location: Basel, Switzerland
Client: Novartis Pharma AG
Architect: Gehry Partners
Principal: Frank O. Gehry, FAIA

P57
Cleveland Clinic Lou Ruvo Center for Brain Health, 2010

Location: Las Vegas
Client: Keep Memory Alive Foundation
Architect: Gehry Partners
Principal: Frank O. Gehry, FAIA

P58–59
Beekman Tower, 2011

Location: New York
Client: Forest City Ratner
Architect: Gehry Partners
Principal: Frank O. Gehry, FAIA

GREG LYNN FORM

P202–3
Korean Presbyterian Church, 1999

Location: Long Island City, New York
Client: Korean Presbyterian Church of New York
Architect: Greg Lynn FORM
Principal: Greg Lynn
Collaborating Architects: Garofalo Architects and Michael McInturf Architects

P205
Bloom House, 2010

Location: Southern California
Client: Jackilin and Jason Bloom
Architect: Greg Lynn FORM
Principal: Greg Lynn
Collaborating Architect:
Lookinglass Architecture & Design

P204
SITE Santa Fe, 2012

Location: Santa Fe, New Mexico
Client: SITE Santa Fe
Architect: Greg Lynn FORM
Principal: Greg Lynn

HODGETTS + FUNG

P127–28
Towell Library, 1992

Location: Los Angeles
Client: University of California, Los
Angeles, UCLA Capital Programs
Architect: Hodgetts + Fung
Principals: Craig Hodgetts, FAIA,
and Hsinming Fung, AIA

P128–29
Sinclaire Pavilion, 2001

Location: Pasadena, California
Client: Art Center College of
Design
Architect: Hodgetts + Fung
Principals: Craig Hodgetts, FAIA,
and Hsinming Fung, AIA

P128
Hyde Park Library, 2004

Location: Los Angeles
Client: Library Facilities Division,
Los Angeles Public Library
Architect: Hodgetts + Fung
Principals: Craig Hodgetts, FAIA,
and Hsinming Fung, AIA

P130
**The Center for Performing Arts,
2009**

Location: Atherton, California
Client: Sequoia Union School
District
Architect: Hodgetts + Fung
Principals: Craig Hodgetts, FAIA,
and Hsinming Fung, AIA

P131
Wild Beast Music Pavilion, 2009

Location: Valencia, California
Client: California Institute of the Arts
Architect: Hodgetts + Fung
Principals: Craig Hodgetts, FAIA,
and Hsinming Fung, AIA

JOHNSTONMARKLEE

P194
Hill House, 2004

Location: Los Angeles
Client: Markee Chautauqua, LLC
Owner: Chan Luu
Architect: JOHNSTONMARKLEE
Principals: Sharon Johnston, AIA,
and Mark Lee

P195
View House, 2009

Location: Rosario, Argentina
Client: Markee Chautauqua, LLC
Architect: JOHNSTONMARKLEE
Principals: Sharon Johnston, AIA,
and Mark Lee
Collaborating Architect: Diego
Arraigada Arquitecto

LORCAN O'HERLIHY
ARCHITECTS

P144–45
Habitat 825, 2007

Location: West Hollywood,
California
Client: Habitat Group LA
Architect: Lorcan O'Herlihy
Architects
Principal: Lorcan O'Herlihy, FAIA

P146
Urban Paramount, 2007

Location: Los Angeles
Client: Urban Environments
Architect: Lorcan O'Herlihy
Architects
Principal: Lorcan O'Herlihy, FAIA

P142–44
Formosa 1140, 2008

Location: West Hollywood,
California
Client: Habitat Group LA
Architect: Lorcan O'Herlihy
Architects
Principal: Lorcan O'Herlihy, FAIA

P144
Willoughby 7917, 2008

Location: West Hollywood,
California
Client: Joshua White, Whitecap
Development, LLC
Architect: Lorcan O'Herlihy
Architects
Principal: Lorcan O'Herlihy, FAIA

P146–47
Flynn Mews House, 2010

Location: Dublin
Client: Ella Flynn
Architect: Lorcan O'Herlihy
Architects
Principal: Lorcan O'Herlihy, FAIA

MAKE
ARCHITECTURE

P185
**Western Car Wash and Retail,
2010**

Location: Torrance, California
Clients: Andrew Kim and Chung Y.
Goh
Architect: MAKE Architecture
Principals: William Beauter, AIA,
and Jess Mullen-Carey

MARK MACK ARCHITECTS

P149
Stremmel Residence, 1992

Location: Reno, Nevada
Clients: Peter and Turkey Stremmel
Architect: Mark Mack Architects
Principal: Mark Mack, AIA

P148
Breitenleerstrasse Housing, 1997

Location: Vienna
Client: Stadt Gemeinde Judenburg
Architect: Mark Mack Architects
Principal: Mark Mack, AIA

P148
Montalvo Art Studios, 1998

Location: Saratoga, California
Client: Montalvo Arts Center
Architect: Mark Mack Architects
Principal: Mark Mack, AIA

P149
Frauengasse Housing, 2004

Location: Judenburg, Austria
Client: DI Feix, Gemeinnuetzige
Wohn-und Siedlungsgenossen-
schaft Ennstal/Liezen
Architect: Mark Mack Architects
Principal: Mark Mack, AIA

P148
AB/BRO, 2007

Location: Los Angeles
Client: Robert Doroux
Architect: Mark Mack Architects
Principal: Mark Mack, AIA

P149
Park Residence, 2009

Location: Laguna Beach, California
Clients: Samuel and Eunna Park
Architect: Mark Mack Architects
Principal: Mark Mack, AIA

MICHAEL MALTZAN ARCHITECTURE

P153
MoMA QNS, 2002

Location: Long Island City, New
York
Client: The Museum of Modern Art
Architect: Michael Maltzan
Architecture
Principal: Michael Maltzan, FAIA

P152–53
Ministructure No. 16, 2006

Location: Jinhua, China
Client: Jinhua City, Jindong New
District
Architect: Michael Maltzan
Architecture
Principal: Michael Maltzan, FAIA

P156
Rainbow Apartments, 2006

Location: Los Angeles
Client: Skid Row Housing Trust
Architect: Michael Maltzan
Architecture
Principal: Michael Maltzan, FAIA

P150–51
Inner-City Arts, 2008

Location: Los Angeles
Client: Inner-City Arts
Architect: Michael Maltzan
Architecture
Principal: Michael Maltzan, FAIA

P154–55
New Carver Apartments, 2009

Location: Los Angeles
Client: Skid Row Housing Trust
Architect: Michael Maltzan
Architecture
Principal: Michael Maltzan, FAIA

P157
Star Apartments, 2013

Location: Los Angeles
Client: Skid Row Housing Trust
Architect: Michael Maltzan
Architecture
Principal: Michael Maltzan, FAIA

P157
**One Santa Fe, 2014 (projected
completion)**

Location: Los Angeles
Client: One Santa Fe, LLC
Architect: Michael Maltzan
Architecture
Principal: Michael Maltzan, FAIA

MORPHOSIS ARCHITECTS

P66
Kate Mantilini Restaurant, 1986

Location: Beverly Hills, California
Clients: Marylin and Harry Lewis
Architect: Morphosis Architects
Principals: Thom Mayne, FAIA, and
Michael Rotondi, FAIA

P66–67
Crawford Residence, 1990

Location: Montecito, California
Clients: Bill and Joan Crawford
Architect: Morphosis Architects
Principals: Thom Mayne, FAIA, and
Michael Rotondi, FAIA

P68
**Salick Health Care Office Building
(8201), 1991**

Location: Los Angeles
Client: Dr. Bernard Salick / Salick
Health Care
Architect: Morphosis Architects
Principals: Thom Mayne, FAIA, and
Michael Rotondi, FAIA

P70–71
Blades Residence, 1997

Location: Santa Barbara, California
Clients: Richard and Vicki Blades
Architect: Morphosis Architects
Principal: Thom Mayne, FAIA

P69
Landa Residence, 1997

Location: Manhattan Beach,
California
Clients: Hans and Jutta Landa
Architect: Morphosis Architects
Principal: Thom Mayne, FAIA

P27, P72–73
Diamond Ranch High School, 1999

Location: Pomona, California
Client: Pomona Unified School District
Architect: Morphosis Architects
Principal: Thom Mayne, FAIA

P74
Hypo Alpe-Adria Center, 2002

Location: Klagenfurt, Austria
Client: Kärntner Landes-und-Hypothekenbank
Architect: Morphosis Architects
Principal: Thom Mayne, FAIA

P25, P78
Caltrans District 7 Headquarters, 2005

Location: Los Angeles
Client: State of California, Department of General Services
Architect: Morphosis Architects
Principal: Thom Mayne, FAIA

P74–75
University of Cincinnati Campus Recreation Center, 2005

Location: Cincinnati
Client: University of Cincinnati
Architect: Morphosis Architects
Principal: Thom Mayne, FAIA

P76–77
Wayne Lyman Morse United States Courthouse, 2006

Location: Eugene, Oregon
Client: United States General Services Administration, Northwest Region 10
Architect: Morphosis Architects
Principal: Thom Mayne, FAIA

P79
San Francisco Federal Building, 2007

Location: San Francisco
Client: United States General Services Administration, Region 9
Architect: Morphosis Architects
Principal: Thom Mayne, FAIA

P80–81
Cahill Center for Astronomy and Astrophysics at Caltech, 2008

Location: Pasadena, California
Client: California Institute of Technology
Architect: Morphosis Architects
Principal: Thom Mayne, FAIA

P81–82
41 Cooper Square, 2009

Location: New York
Client: The Cooper Union for the Advancement of Science and Art
Architect: Morphosis Architects
Principal: Thom Mayne, FAIA

P83
Phare Tower, 2017 (projected completion)

Location: Paris
Client: SCI CNIT Developpement
Architect: Morphosis Architects
Principal: Thom Mayne, FAIA

NEIL M. DENARI ARCHITECTS

P158
L.A. Eyeworks, 2002

Location: Los Angeles
Clients: Gai Gherardi and Barbara McReynolds
Architect: Neil M. Denari Architects
Principal: Neil M. Denari, AIA

P158–59
Alan-Voo House, 2007

Location: Los Angeles
Clients: Eric Alan and Rhonda Voo
Architect: Neil M. Denari Architects
Principal: Neil M. Denari, AIA

P160–61
HL23, 2011

Location: New York
Clients: Garrett Heher and Alf Naman
Architect: Neil M. Denari Architects
Principal: Neil M. Denari, AIA

PATRICK TIGHE ARCHITECTURE

P200
Collins Gallery, 2001

Location: West Hollywood, California
Client: Michael Collins
Architect: Patrick Tighe Architecture
Principal: Patrick Tighe, FAIA

P200
Live Oak Studio, 2006

Location: Los Angeles
Client: Steve Werndorf
Architect: Patrick Tighe Architecture
Principal: Patrick Tighe, FAIA

P198
Ashcroft Writer's Studio, 2007

Location: West Hollywood, California
Client: Paola Peroni
Architect: Patrick Tighe Architecture
Principal: Patrick Tighe, FAIA

P201
Gelner Residence, 2008

Location: Mar Vista, California
Clients: Kendra and William Gelner
Architect: Patrick Tighe Architecture
Principal: Patrick Tighe, FAIA

P8, P199
Tigertail Residence, 2008

Location: Los Angeles
Client: Hugh MacDonald
Architect: Patrick Tighe Architecture
Principal: Patrick Tighe, FAIA

P198–99
Sierra Bonita Mixed Use Affordable Housing, 2010

Location: West Hollywood, California
Clients: West Hollywood Community Housing Corporation and the City of West Hollywood
Architect: Patrick Tighe Architecture
Principal: Patrick Tighe, FAIA

P123
La Brea Affordable Housing, 2013

Location: Los Angeles
Clients: West Hollywood
Community Housing Corporation
and the City of West Hollywood
Architect: Patrick Tighe Architecture
Principal: Patrick Tighe, FAIA
Collaborating Architect: John V.
Mutlow, FAIA

P-A-T-T-E-R-N-S

P181–83
FyF Residence, 2009

Location: Rosario, Argentina
Clients: Florencia and Fernando
Garcia
Architect: P-A-T-T-E-R-N-S
Principals: Marcelo Spina and
Georgina Huljich

P16
Prism Gallery, 2009

Location: West Hollywood,
California
Client: Elite Property Management
Architect: P-A-T-T-E-R-N-S
Principals: Marcelo Spina and
Georgina Huljich

P184
Jujuy Redux, 2011

Location: Rosario, Argentina
Client: DRS Construcciones S.A.
Architect: P-A-T-T-E-R-N-S
Principals: Marcelo Spina and
Georgina Huljich
Collaborating Architect: Maxi
Spina Architects

PREDOCK FRANE ARCHITECTS

P190–91
Habitat 15, 2009

Location: Los Angeles
Client: Habitat Group LA
Architect: Predock Frane Architects
Principals: Hadrian Predock, AIA,
and John Frane

P191
Venice House, 2012

Location: Los Angeles
Clients: David Elworthy and Ellen
Bridle
Architect: Predock Frane Architects
Principals: Hadrian Predock, AIA,
and John Frane

RANDALL STOUT ARCHITECTS

P133
Blair Graphics, 2000

Location: Santa Monica, California
Client: Robert N. Blair, president,
Blair Graphics
Architect: Randall Stout Architects
Principal: Randall Stout, FAIA

P132–33
**Steinhüde Sea Recreation Facility,
2000**

Location: Steinhüde, Germany
Client: Elektrizitätswerk Minden-
Ravensberg GmbH
Architect: Randall Stout Architects
Principal: Randall Stout, FAIA

ROTO ARCHITECTS

P93
CDLT 1, 2, 1992

Location: Los Angeles
Client: Rotondi Family
Architect: RoTo Architects
Principal: Michael Rotondi, FAIA

P93
New Jersey House, 1996

Location: Bernardsville, New Jersey
Client: David Teiger
Architect: RoTo Architects
Principal: Michael Rotondi, FAIA

P94–95
Carlson-Reges House, 1996

Location: Los Angeles
Clients: Kathy Reges and Richard
Carlson
Architect: RoTo Architects
Principal: Michael Rotondi, FAIA

P95
Warehouse C, 1997

Location: Nagasaki, Japan
Client: Governor Isamu Takada
Architect: RoTo Architects
Principal: Michael Rotondi, FAIA

P96–97
**Architecture and Art Building,
Prairie View A & M University, 2005**

Location: Prairie View, Texas
Client: Prairie View A & M University
Architect: RoTo Architects
Principal: Michael Rotondi, FAIA

P97
**Madame Tussauds Hollywood,
2009**

Location: Los Angeles
Client: Madame Tussauds
Architect: RoTo Architects
Principal: Michael Rotondi, FAIA
Collaborating Architect: JAG
Architects

SAEE STUDIO

P98
Angeli Trattoria, 1986

Location: Los Angeles
Clients: Evan Kleiman and John
Strobel
Architect: Saee Studio
Principal: Michele Saee

P98
434 Apartments, 1989

Location: Los Angeles
Client: Building Inc.
Architect: Saee Studio
Principal: Michele Saee

P99
Linnie House, 2004

Location: Los Angeles
Clients: Shelly Berger and Lothar Schmitz
Architect: Saee Studio
Principal: Michele Saee

P98–99
Publicis Drugstore, 2004

Location: Paris
Client: Publicis Drugstore
Architect: Saee Studio
Principal: Michele Saee

STUDIO WORKS ARCHITECTS

P134
Pilibos School Library and Gymnasium, 2006

Location: Los Angeles
Clients: Rose and Alex Pilibos Armenian School, Western Prelacy of the Armenian Apostolic Church of America
Architect: Studio Works Architects
Principals: Robert Mangurian and Mary-Ann Ray

TOURAINE RICHMOND ARCHITECTS

P196
One Window House, 2005

Location: Los Angeles
Clients: Olivier Touraine and Deborah Richmond
Architect: Touraine Richmond Architects
Principals: Olivier Touraine and Deborah Richmond, AIA

P197
Plug and Play House, 2008

Location: Minneapolis
Clients: Noriko Gamblin and Steven Ostrow
Architect: Touraine Richmond Architects
Principals: Olivier Touraine and Deborah Richmond, AIA

VOID

P110
Bobco Metals Co., 2004

Location: Los Angeles
Client: Bobco Metals Co.
Architect: VOID
Principal: Arshia Mahmoodi
Design Collaboration: Reza Bagherzadeh

P111
Mulholland Residence, 2011

Location: Los Angeles
Client: Naghemeh Khoshnoud
Architect: VOID
Principal: Arshia Mahmoodi

WARREN TECHENTIN ARCHITECTURE

P9, P192–93
Los Feliz Residence 1, 2008

Location: Los Angeles
Clients: Warren and Mimi Techentin
Architect: Warren Techentin Architecture
Principal: Warren Techentin, AIA

P193
Montrose Duplex, 2010

Location: Montrose, California
Clients: Daniel and Tracy Hurley
Architect: Warren Techentin Architecture
Principal: Warren Techentin, AIA

XTEN ARCHITECTURE

P164–65
Surfhouse, 2007

Location: Hermosa Beach, California
Clients: Jennifer and Nick Hall
Architect: XTEN Architecture
Principals: Monika Häfelfinger, SIA, and Austin Kelly, AIA

P167
Diamondhouse, 2009
Location: Santa Monica, California
Client: Aisha Ayers
Architect: XTEN Architecture
Principals: Monika Häfelfinger, SIA, and Austin Kelly AIA

P166–67
Sapphire Gallery, 2009

Location: Los Angeles
Clients: Frederick and Julie Reisz
Architect: XTEN Architecture
Principals: Monika Häfelfinger, SIA, and Austin Kelly, AIA

P4, P121
Nakahouse, 2010

Location: Los Angeles
Clients: Ryan Burns and Aline Nakashima
Architect: XTEN Architecture
Principals: Monika Häfelfinger, SIA, and Austin Kelly, AIA

Selected Bibliography

"An Hour with Architect Thom Mayne." Interview with Thom Mayne. *Charlie Rose.* December 2, 2005. http://www.charlierose.com/view/interview/636.

Architectures Expérimentales, 1950–2000. Orléans: Editions HYX, 2003.

Armstrong, Richard. *Sculpture in California, 1975–80: An Exhibition.* San Diego: The Museum, 1980.

Banham, Reyner. *Los Angeles: The Architecture of Four Ecologies.* New York: Harper & Row, 1971.

———. *The New Brutalism: Ethic or Aesthetic?* London: Architectural Press, 1966.

Banham, Reyner, and Mary Banham. *A Critic Writes: Essays by Reyner Banham.* Berkeley: University of California Press, 1999.

Barron, Stephanie, Sheri Bernstein, and Ilene S. Fort. *Reading California: Art, Image, and Identity, 1900–2000.* Los Angeles: Los Angeles County Museum of Art, 2000.

Betsky, Aaron. "Architecture: Steel Chic and Stucco Dreams at the L.A. Lab." *Metropolitan Home* 21, no. 8 (August 1989): 75, 77–87.

———. *Drager House: Franklin D. Israel.* London: Phaidon, 1996.

———. *Violated Perfection: Architecture and the Fragmentation of the Modern.* New York: Rizzoli, 1990.

Betsky, Aaron, John Chase, and Leon Whiteson. *Experimental Architecture in Los Angeles.* New York: Rizzoli, 1991.

Boissière, Olivier. "Ten California Architects." *Domus* 604 (March 1980) [The young architects of California]: 17–31.

California Sculpture Show. Los Angeles: California/International Arts Foundation, 1984.

Chamberlain, John, Julie Sylvester, and Klaus Kertess. *John Chamberlain: A Catalogue Raisonné of the Sculpture 1954–1985.* New York: Hudson Hills Press, 1986.

Chase, John. *LA 2000+: New Architecture in Los Angeles.* New York: Monacelli Press, 2006.

Cohen, Jean-Louis, John Lautner, Nicholas Olsberg, and Frank Escher. *Between Earth and Heaven: The Architecture of John Lautner.* New York: Rizzoli, 2008.

Conner, Bruce, Gerald Matt, Barbara Steffen, and Peter W. Boswell. *Bruce Conner: The 70s.* Vienna: Kunsthalle Wien, 2010.

Cuff, Dana. *The Provisional City: Los Angeles Stories of Architecture and Urbanism.* Cambridge, Mass.: MIT Press, 2000.

Dal Co, Francesco, Frank O. Gehry, Kurt W. Forster, and Hadley S. Arnold. *Frank O. Gehry: The Complete Works.* New York: Monacelli Press, 1998.

Davis, Mike. *City of Quartz: Excavating the Future in Los Angeles.* London: Verso, 1990.

———. *Ecology of Fear: Los Angeles and the Imagination of Disaster.* New York: Metropolitan Books, 1998.

Denari, Neil M. *Gyroscopic Horizons.* New York: Princeton Architectural Press, 1999.

Dixon, John Morris. "The Santa Monica School: What's Its Lasting Contribution?." *Progressive Architecture* (March 1995): 63–71, 112,114.

———. "Superstructure." *Progressive Architecture* (July 1995): 60–69.

Dreyfuss, John. "Gallery Stirs Up Architects." *Los Angeles Times* (December 12, 1979).

Elaine, James, Aimee Chang, and Christopher Miles. *Thing: New Sculpture from Los Angeles.* Los Angeles: Hammer Museum, 2005.

Emerging Voices: A New Generation of Architects in America. New York: Architectural League of New York, 1986.

Foster, Hal. *The Art-Architecture Complex.* London: Verso, 2011.

———. "Why All the Hoopla?." Review of *Frank Gehry: The Art of Architecture,* edited by Jean-Louis Cohen et al. *London Review of Books* 23, no. 16 (August 23, 2001): 24–26. http://www.lrb.co.uk/v23/n16/hal-foster/why-all-the-hoopla.

Friedman, Mildred S., and Michael Sorkin. *Gehry Talks: Architecture + Process.* New York: Rizzoli, 1999.

Gebhard, David, and Robert Winter. *A Guide to Architecture in Southern California.* Los Angeles: Los Angeles County Museum of Art, 1965.

———. *Architecture in Los Angeles: A Complete Guide.* Salt Lake City: Gibbs Smith, 1985.

———. *Los Angeles, An Architectural Guide.* Salt Lake City: Gibbs Smith, 1994.

Gebhard, David, and Breton H. Von. *Lloyd Wright, Architect: 20th Century Architecture in an Organic Exhibition.* Santa Barbara, Calif.: Santa Barbara Art Gallery, 1971.

Gehry, Frank O. SCI-Arc lecture, with introduction by Ray Kappe. SCI-Arc Media Archive. January 1, 1975. http://sma.sciarc.edu/video/frank-o-gehry-1-of-2.

———. *Frank O. Gehry: The Architect's Studio: August 18–November 12, 2000.* Seattle: Henry Art Gallery, 2000.

Gehry, Frank O., Peter Arnell, Ted Bickford, Germano Celant, and Mason Andrews. *Frank Gehry, Buildings and Projects.* New York: Rizzoli, 1985.

Gehry, Frank O., and Rosemarie H. Bletter. *The Architecture of Frank Gehry.* New York: Rizzoli, 1986.

Gehry, Frank O., Kurt W. Forster, and Cristina Bechtler. *Frank O. Gehry, Kurt W. Forster.* Ostfildern-Ruit, Germany: Hatje Cantz Verlag, 1999.

Gehry, Frank O., and Brooke Hodge. *F.O.G: Flowing in All Directions.* Los Angeles: CIRCA Pub., 2003.

Gehry, Frank O., and Richard Koshalek. *Symphony: Frank Gehry's Walt Disney Concert Hall.* New York: Harry N. Abrams in association with the Los Angeles Philharmonic, 2003.

Gehry, Frank O., Bill Lacy, and Susan deMenil. *Angels & Franciscans: Innovative Architecture from Los Angeles and San Francisco.* New York: Rizzoli, 1992.

Ghirardo, Diane Y., and Mark Mack. *Mark Mack: A California Architect.* Tübingen, Germany: Wasmuth, 1994.

Giaconia, Paola. *Eric Owen Moss: The Uncertainty of Doing.* Milan: Skira, 2006.

Giovannini, Joseph. "For a New Los Angeles Style, A Place in the Sun." *The New York Times* (April 16, 1987).

Goldberger, Paul. "Houses as Art; The Masterpieces They Call Home." *The New York Times* (March 12, 1995).

Gudis, Catherine, Mary J. Jacob, and Ann Goldstein. *A Forest of Signs: Art in the Crisis of Representation.* Cambridge, Mass.: MIT Press, 1989.

Hawthorne, Christopher. "Reading L.A.: Charles Jencks on Frank Gehry, Thom Mayne, and the rest of the L.A. School." *Los Angeles Times* (July 29, 2011).

Herms, George. *George Herms: Then and Now, Fifty Years of Assemblage.* Philadelphia: Seraphin Gallery, 2002.

Hess, Alan, John Lautner, and Alan Weintraub. *The Architecture of John Lautner.* New York: Rizzoli, 1999.

Hodgetts, Craig. *Hodgetts + Fung: Scenarios and Spaces.* New York: Rizzoli, 1997.

Isenberg, Barbara, and Frank O. Gehry. *Conversations with Frank Gehry.* New York: Alfred A. Knopf, 2009.

Israel, Franklin D., and Frank O. Gehry. *Franklin D. Israel: Buildings and Projects.* New York: Rizzoli, 1992.

Jencks, Charles. *Architecture 2000: Predictions and Methods.* New York: Praeger, 1971.

———. *Daydream Houses of Los Angeles.* New York: Rizzoli, 1978.

———. *Heteropolis: Los Angeles, the Riots and the Strange Beauty of Hetero-Architecture.* London: Academy Editions, 1993.

———. *The New Paradigm in Architecture: The Language of Postmodernism.* New Haven, Conn.: Yale University Press, 2002.

Jencks, Charles, and Nathan Silver. *Adhocism: The Case for Improvisation.* New York: Doubleday, 1972.

Jodidio, Philip. *Architecture in the United States: Us.* Cologne: Taschen, 2006.

———. *Architecture Now!* Cologne: Taschen, 2002.

———. *Contemporary California Architects*. Cologne: Taschen, 1995.

———. *New Forms: Architecture in the 1990s*. Cologne: Taschen, 2001.

Kipnis, Jeffrey. "Who Is Moss?" SCI-Arc special lecture. March 6, 2012. SCI-Arc Media Archive. http://www.sciarc.edu/lectures.php?id=2055.

Koshalek, Richard, Dana Hutt, Thom Mayne, and Frances Anderton. *L.A. Now*. Pasadena, Calif.: Art Center College of Design, 2001.

Lee, Joon-hee, and Doo-sik Shin. *B + U: Herwig Baumgartner, Scott Uriu*. Seoul: Equal Books, 2011.

Lubell, Sam. *Living West: New Residential Architecture in Southern California*. New York: Monacelli Press, 2009.

Lynn, Greg. *Folds, Bodies & Blobs: Collected Essays*. Brussels: La Lettre volée, 1998.

———. *Animate Form*. New York: Princeton Architectural Press, 1999.

———. *Folding in Architecture*. Chichester, England: Wiley-Academy, 2004.

Lynn, Greg, and Mark Gage. *Composites, Surfaces, and Software: High Performance Architecture*. New Haven, Conn.: Yale School of Architecture, 2010.

Lynn, Greg, and Mark Rappolt. *Greg Lynn Form*. New York: Rizzoli, 2008.

Mack, Mark. *Stremmel House: Mark Mack*. New York: Monacelli Press, 1997.

Maltzan, Michael, and Jessica Varner. *No More Play: Conversations on Urban Speculation in Los Angeles and Beyond*. Ostfildern-Ruit, Germany: Hatje Cantz Verlag, 2011.

Martin, Richard. *The New Urban Landscape*. New York: Olympia & York Companies, 1990.

Mayne, Thom. *The Continuity of Contradiction*. Buffalo N.Y.: School of Architecture and Planning, 2010.

Mayne, Thom, Jeffrey Kipnis, and Todd Gannon. *Morphosis/Diamond Ranch High School, Diamond Bar, California*. New York: Monacelli Press, 2001.

Mayne, Thom, and Val K. Warke. *Morphosis*. London: Phaidon, 2003.

Mayne, Thom, and Peter Cook. *Fresh Morphosis 1998–2004*. New York: Rizzoli, 2006.

McCoy, Esther. *Case Study Houses, 1945–1962*. Los Angeles: Hennessey & Ingalls, 1977.

———. *The Second Generation*. Salt Lake City: Peregrine Smith Books, 1984.

McCoy, Esther, R. M. Schindler, Richard J. Neutra, and Louis H. Sullivan. *Vienna to Los Angeles: Two Journeys*. Santa Monica, Calif.: Arts + Architecture Press, 1979.

McMakin, Roy, Paul Goldberger, and Grant Mudford. "Architecture: Frank Israel: Reinventing the California Ranch House for the Hills of Malibu." *Architectural Digest* 53, no. 12 (1996): 156.

Meyer, Esther C. *Frank Gehry: On Line*. Princeton, N.J.: Princeton University Art Museum, 2008.

Migayrou, Frédéric. *Morphosis: Continuities of the Incomplete*. Paris: Centre Pompidou, 2006.

Moneo, José R. *Theoretical Anxiety and Design Strategies in the Work of Eight Contemporary Architects*. Cambridge, Mass.: MIT Press, 2004.

Moss, Eric Owen. *Eric Owen Moss*. London: Academy Editions, 1993.

———. *Eric Owen Moss Construction Manual, 1988–2008*. Beijing: AADCU, 2009.

———. *Gnostic Architecture*. New York: Monacelli Press, 1999.

———. *SCI-Arc Gallery 2002–10*. Beijing: AADCU, 2010.

Moss, Eric Owen, Preston S. Cohen, Brooke Hodge, Andrew Bush, Herbert Muschamp, and Peter G. Rowe. *Eric Owen Moss: The Box*. Cambridge, Mass.: Harvard University Graduate School of Design, 1995.

Moss, Eric Owen., and Julianna Morais. *Who Says What Architecture Is?* Los Angeles: SCI-Arc Press, 2007.

Muschamp, Herbert. "A City Poised on Glitter and Ashes." *The New York Times* (March 10, 1996).

Leonardi, Nicola. *New Forms: Plans and Details for Contemporary Architects*. London: Thames & Hudson, 2009.

Ouroussoff, Nicolai. "Designed to Help Uplift the Poor." *The New York Times* (February 18, 2010).

———. "Neil Denari; Striking a Balance between Avant-Garde and Practical Architecture." *Los Angeles Times* (August 17, 1997).

———. "Two Schools of Thought; Camino Nuevo Elementary: The Mini-Mall Recycled to Embrace Students from Diverse Backgrounds Affirms the Social Impact of Design." *Los Angeles Times* (November 1, 2000).

Ragheb, J. Fiona, Frank O. Gehry, Jean-Louis Cohen, and Mildred S. Friedman. *Frank Gehry, Architect*. New York: Guggenheim Museum Publications, 2001.

Rauterberg, Hanno. *Talking Architecture: Interviews with Architects*. Munich: Prestel, 2008.

Richardson, Sara. *Morphosis: Thom Mayne and Michael Rotondi*. Monticello, Ill.: Vance Bibliographies, 1986.

Rieff, David. *Los Angeles: Capital of the Third World*. New York: Simon & Schuster, 1991.

Rosa, Joseph, and Hernan Alonso Díaz. *Xefirotarch*. San Francisco: San Francisco Museum of Modern Art, 2006.

Rotondi, Michael, and Clark P. Stevens. *Roto Works: Stillpoints*. New York: Rizzoli, 2006.

Rubins, Nancy. *Nancy Rubins*. San Diego: Museum of Contemporary Art, 1995.

Ryan, Raymund, Michael Maltzan, Ai Weiwei, and Mirko Zardini. *Michael Maltzan: Alternate Ground*. Pittsburgh: Heinz Architectural Center, Carnegie Museum of Art, 2005.

Saee, Michele, Aris Janigian, and Frédéric Migayrou. *Michele Saee: Buildings + Projects*. New York: Rizzoli, 1997.

Scott, Allen J., and Edward W. Soja. *The City: Los Angeles and Urban Theory at the End of the Twentieth Century*. Berkeley: University of California Press, 1998.

Smith, Elizabeth A. T., and Russell Ferguson. *Urban Revisions: Current Projects for the Public Realm*. Los Angeles: Museum of Contemporary Art, 1994.

Smith, Elizabeth A. T., and Esther McCoy. *Blueprints for Modern Living: History and Legacy of the Case Study Houses*. Los Angeles: Museum of Contemporary Art, 1989.

Smith, Elizabeth A. T., Julius Shulman, and Peter Goessel. *Case Study Houses*. Cologne: Taschen, 2002.

"Southern California Architectural History: Blog for fans of the architectural and design history of Southern California and related published material." http://socalarchhistory.blogspot.com/2010/04/frederick-fisher-and-venice-rat-pack.html.

Spina, Marcelo, and Georgina Huljich. *Patterns Embedded*. Beijing: Beijing Office/United Asia Art & Design Cooperation, 2011.

Steele, James. *Los Angeles Architecture: The Contemporary Condition*. London: Phaidon, 1993.

Steele, James, and Aaron Betsky. *Contemporary California Houses: Frank Gehry: Schnabel House; Eric Owen Moss: Lawson-Westen House; Franklin D. Israel: Drager House*. London: Phaidon, 1999.

Steele, James, and Eric Owen Moss. *Lawson-Westen House: Eric Owen Moss*. London: Phaidon, 1995.

Stella, Frank, and Paul Goldberger. *Frank Stella: Painting into Architecture*. New York: Metropolitan Museum of Art, 2007.

Stout, Randall. *Environmental Alchemy: Randall Stout Architects*. New York: Edizioni Press, 2004.

Stout, Randall, Jon Coddington, and Judy L. Larson. *Design Peak: Randall Stout*. Seoul: Equal Books, 2010.

Street-Porter, Tim. *Freestyle: The New Architecture and Interior Design from Los Angeles*. New York: Stewart, Tabori & Chang, 1986.

Tennent, Scott. *Jones, Partners: Architecture: El Segundo: Designs for Words, Buildings: Machines*. New York: Princeton Architectural Press, 2007.

Venturi, Robert. *Complexity and Contradiction in Architecture: With an Introduction by Vincent Scully*. New York: Museum of Modern Art, 1966.

Voulkos, Peter, Rose Slivka, and Karen Tsujimoto. *The Art of Peter Voulkos*. Tokyo: Kodansha International in collaboration with the Oakland Museum, 1995.

Waldman, Diane. *Collage, Assemblage, and the Found Object*. New York: Harry N. Abrams, 1992.

Walker, Stephen, and Gordon Matta-Clark. *Gordon Matta-Clark: Art, Architecture and the Attack on Modernism*. London: I. B. Tauris, 2009.

Whiteson, Leon. "Kentucky Fried Changes: Architecture: Is there any reason why all the Colonel's chicken emporiums should look alike? One owner thought not, so he hired a team to design something radically different." *Los Angeles Times* (July 5, 1990).

———. "L.A.'s New-Wave Designers Draw Global Attention." *Los Angeles Times* (July 11, 1989).

Wigley, Mark. *The Architecture of Deconstruction: Derrida's Haunt*. Cambridge, Mass.: MIT Press, 1993.

Zellner, Peter. *Hybrid Space: New Forms in Digital Architecture*. New York: Rizzoli, 1999.

Index

Photo Credits

Photographs appear courtesy of the artist, architectural firm, or institution named in the accompanying captions unless otherwise indicated below. Every effort has been made to contact all copyright holders.

Copyright © Roland Halbe, pp. 2–3, 25, 52–53, 74, 75 (center and right), 78, 80–81 (top); photo: Steve King, p. 4; © John Ellis, pp. 5, 135 (top left and right); courtesy Ball-Nogues Studio, © Neil Cochran, p. 7; photo: Art Gray, pp. 8, 120 (right), 122 (right), 164 (top and bottom on right), 165–67, 176 (left), 198–201; © Eric Staudenmaier, pp. 9, 192, 193 (top left), 194; photo: Iwan Baan, pp. 10, 57, 79, 81 (bottom), 82, 150–52 (top and bottom on left, right), 154–55, 162–63; © Tom Bonner, pp. 11, 24, 27–28, 61, 68–69 (bottom), 100–7, 109 (top), 119 (right), 120 (left), 130–31, 136 (left and center); © Joshua White/ JWPictures, pp. 12, 40 (right), 41 (left), 133 (top and bottom), 168 (left), 175 (left), 206–7; © Nic Lehoux, pp. 13, 77 (top); © Jason Schmidt, pp. 14, 141; © Fotoworks/Benny Chan, pp. 17, 110 (top), 116 (right), 117 (right), 118 (left and right), 128 (botom left), 137, 158–61, 170 (left), 193 (bottom left), 211; © 2012 Tim Griffith, pp. 18–19, 138, 140; © Grant Mudford, pp. 21, 33 (right), 34 (left), 39 (right), 62–65 (left and top right), 88, 134 (top and bottom on left, and bottom right); © Johanna Vandemoortele, p. 117 (left); © Bruce Damonte, pp. 26, 121 (left), 139; photo: Brandon Welling, courtesy of Morphosis Architects, pp. 30 (left), 69 (top), 71 (top); © Scott Mayoral, pp. 30 (top right), 179 (middle), 212, 214–15; © Kienholz, courtesy L.A. Louver, Venice, CA, photo courtesy of Whitney Museum of American Art, New York, photography by Sheldon C. Collins, p. 32 (left); courtesy of the Ken Price Studio, © Fredrik Nilsen, p. 32 (right); © Ave Pildas, p. 33 (left); dbox, a creative & branding agency, pp. 38 (left), 58–59; courtesy of Larry Bell, photo: Eric Sutherland for Walker Art Center, Minneapolis, p. 38 (right); © Jack Laxer, Pacific Palisades, California, p. 40 (left); © Timothy Swope, pp. 41 (right), 65 (bottom right); courtesy of Guggenheim Museum Bilbao, 1997, David Heald © The Solomon R. Guggneheim Foundation, New York, p. 45; © 1993 Don F. Wong, p. 47; photo: thomasmayerarchive.com, pp. 48, 50, 55–56; © Timothy Hursley, pp. 51, 116 (left), 123 (right), 208–9; © Klemens Ortmayer, pp. 54 (left); Tim Street-Porter, pp. 60, 85 (right); © Tim Street-Porter/Esto, p. 66 (top left); © Kim Zwarts, pp. 66 (bottom and top right), 67, 70, 71 (bottom), 72, 73 (bottom), 74 (top and bottom); © Steve Proehl, p. 73 (top); © Frank Ooms, p. 76; © Tim Griffith/Esto, p. 77 (bottom); courtesy of the University of California, on behalf of the USC Special Collections, photo: Dick Whittington Studio, p. 84 (right); © Joe Mabel, p. 85 (left); © Saee Studio, photo: Tim Street-Porter, p. 98 (top left); © Saee Studio, photo: Luc Boegly, p. 98 (right); © Saee Studio, photo: Marvin Rand, p. 98 (bottom left), 99 (top and bottom on right); courtesy of Los Angeles Almanac @ LA Almanac.com, p. 86 (left); © Marvin Rand Estate, pp. 86 (right), 129, 186–88 (top and bottom on left); courtesy of the Richard and Dione Neutra Collection, College of Environmental Design, Special Collection, California State Polytechnic University, Pomona,

Luckhaus photo, p. 87 (right); courtesy of the Architecture and Design Collection, University Art Museum, University of California, Santa Barbara, p. 87 (left); © David Zanzinger, p. 89; © Tara Wujcik p. 110 (bottom); © Imeh Akpanudosen, p. 111 (bottom); © Paul Warchol, p. 114 (left); © David Travers, pp. 115 (right), 216 (right), 217 (left), 220–21 (left); © Peter Hubbe, pp. 132 (top, bottom, and right); © Lawrence Anderson, pp. 142–45, 174 (left); © Alice Clancy, pp. 146 (top), 147; © 2007 Tate Lown, p. 146 (bottom); © AnnA BlaU, p. 148 (bottom right); © Manfred Seidl, pp. 148 (bottom left), 149 (bottom); © Richard Barnes, p. 148 (top right); © Christian Richters, p. 153 (top and bottom on right); photo: Erhard Pfeiffer, pp. 168 (top and bottom on right), 169; © Ben Cope, p. 174 (far right); photo: John Edward Linden, pp. 185, 189; © Elon Schoenholz, p. 190 (top and right); © Nicolas O. S. Marques/PHOTEKT, p. 191; © Nicholas Alan Cope, p. 193 (right); © Sergio Pirrone, p. 195 (top); © Gustavo Frittegotto, p. 195 (bottom); © Karen Melvin Photography, pp.196–97; © Ari Marcopoulos, pp. 202–03 (bottom); © Richard Schulman, p. 203 (top); © Richard Powers, p. 205; © Oliver Hess, p. 210; © Mark Lentz, p. 213 (top); © Steph Goralnick, p. 213 (bottom); © Alan Weintraub/Arcaid/Corbis, pp. 216 (left), 221 (right); courtesy The Museum of Modern Art | Avery Architectural & Fine Arts Library, Columbia University, New York, © 2012 Frank Lloyd Wright Foundation, Scottsdale, AZ/Artists Rights Society (ARS), NY, pp. 217 (right), 218 (left); courtesy of Harwell Hamilton Harris Papers, Alexander Architectural Archive, The University of Texas Libraries, The University of Texas at Austin, pp. 218 (right), 219 (left); courtesy of Harwell Hamilton Harris Papers, Alexander Architectural Archive, The University of Texas Libraries, The University of Texas at Austin, photo © 2012 Man Ray Trust/Artists Rights Society (ARS), New York/ADAGP, Paris, p. 219 (right); courtesy The Museum of Contemporary Art, Los Angeles, p. 222 (left); courtesy of Hodgetts + Fung, © 2012 Eames Office LLC (eamesoffice.com), p. 222 (right); and courtesy of Hodgetts + Fung, © 2012 Eames Office LLC (eamesoffice.com), photo © 2012 Museum Associates/LACMA, p. 223.